Musical Interpretation

by
Jack Westrup

BRITISH BROADCASTING CORPORATION

This book accompanies a series
of BBC radio programmes
first broadcast on Radio 3 (Study),
weekly on Thursdays at 7 p.m.
from April 1 to June 3 1971

Contents

Interpretation can have several related meanings. The Latin word *interpres* meant originally an agent or go-between, and hence someone who explains or expounds and more particularly someone who translates remarks made in a foreign language. In modern English the word 'interpreter' commonly means one who acts as a *viva voce* translator. But we can also speak of someone interpreting the Scriptures by means of a spoken or written commentary, and we also say: 'I don't know how to interpret that' – meaning that the implication of a statement is not completely clear. In music, as in literature, interpretation can mean exposition, though it is more usual to speak of 'analysis'. But the meaning with which we are particularly concerned here relates to performance. A performer, like an actor, is an intermediary between the composer or author and the public. It is quite possible to read a play at home or in the school-room, and many musicians derive pleasure from reading music without hearing it. But just as drama is designed for the stage and does not properly come alive till it is acted, so music is meant to be performed and strictly speaking does not exist until it is heard. If we sit in a chair and read music we are, in fact, imagining a performance and interpreting the music for ourselves.

It is obvious that the interpretation of music presents serious problems. Ideally we want to hear what the composer intended, but this is not always easy to discover. One might expect that composers would be the best interpreters of their own music, but this is not necessarily so – partly, no doubt, because they are absorbed in what they originally imagined and hence pay insufficient attention to what they are hearing. They may ignore their own precise indications of speed, or they may change the speed from one performance to another, particularly as they grow older. There is no such thing as a faithful performance, since it is impossible to know exactly to what it should be faithful. In the last resort the interpreter has to rely on taste and judgment, and these are not easy to define. It is clear that an interpreter must understand what he is performing and must be sympathetic towards it; but it is too much to expect that he should submerge his own personality completely. If his personality dominates the performance we get a wilful interpretation, which does neither the composer nor the public any service. If, on the other hand, his personality is dormant the result will be colourless to the point of tedium.

Notation

His first task, however, is to get the notes right. This might seem a relatively simple matter. Unfortunately the written notation of music has never been sufficiently precise to indicate everything that the composer had in mind, or that he might think desirable. Every sensitive performer instinctively makes minute fluctuations of dynamics, rhythm and tempo which cannot be recorded on paper – or if the attempt were made to record them the result would be artificial. As we shall see later, twentieth-century composers have often gone into considerable detail to make their intentions clear; but the most precise indications still leave something to the performer's imagination. If we go back into the past, the difficulties of interpreting notation increase considerably. One of the reasons for this is that composers were writing for performers familiar with the conventions of the period and so allowed a good deal to be taken for granted. Another is that notation becomes more precise in detail only when the need for such precision arises.

A particular instance is the plainsong of the Catholic Church. In the early centuries of the Christian era, so far as we can tell, this was transmitted orally. But with the spread of the Church through Western Europe it must have been felt that some way of recording the music was necessary. The first step was taken by adapting the signs used for Greek accents and combining them when necessary. These signs gave a general idea of where the tune went up or down but could hardly serve as more than a reminder to singers who had already learned it. Some indications of interpretation were added in the shape of letters, e.g. *c* = *celeriter* (quickly), *x* = *expectare* (to wait). But as an early twelfth-century writer pointed out, not only were the signs vague but the letters could be too: *l*, for instance, could stand either for *leniter* (smoothly) or for *lugubriter* (mournfully). In the tenth century an attempt was made to define the relative pitch of notes more accurately by drawing a line across the page. From this it was a natural step to draw several lines across the page and to identify them by reference to the letters by which the notes were known. If one of the lines was marked C or F, for instance, the pitch of the other lines, and the spaces between them, was also known. This was the origin of the staff notation which we still use. The question of rhythm, however, remained undefined and is still a matter of controversy. Early medieval writers distinguish between 'long' and 'short' notes, but it is not clear whether this implies an exact mathematical relationship. Later

writers make a distinction between 'measured music', by which they mean polyphonic music, and plainsong. The two views are not irreconcilable. Since the texts of plainsong, apart from hymns and similar compositions, are in prose there is clearly no need for a strictly metrical interpretation. In any case, it would seem probable that methods of singing plainsong differed at different times and in different countries.

As soon as composers started writing music for two or more voices simultaneously, difficulties of interpretation were liable to arise. So long as the two voices moved strictly together there was no more need to define the rhythm than there was in plainsong, since in the thirteenth century, and earlier, polyphonic music (music for several voices) was sung not by the full choir but by soloists. But if the movement of the voices was more elaborate some means had to be found to give them rhythmical definition. This was done by grouping notes together in such a way that they would imply a precise rhythmical interpretation. The nature of the

Cantors of the *Volto Santo*   *Amico Aspertini, 1506*

groups would determine the time or rhythm, which would be persistent. *Example 1* (from the thirteenth century) illustrates this type of notation and provides a transcription into modern notation.

The long note in the lowest part is the first note of an antiphon sung before and after the 'Magnificat' on the feast of St. John the Evangelist (27 December): *'Exiit sermo inter fratres, quod discipulus ille non moritur'* (Then went this saying abroad among the brethren, that that disciple should not die: St. John, xxi, 23). The succeeding notes of the antiphon are sustained in the same way. Since it would be difficult for a singer to sustain a note for so long it is possible that these long notes were played on the organ. If we accept this and also accept the rhythmical interpretation of the upper parts, there are still problems for the modern performer. How fast was the music meant to be sung? What sort of tone did thirteenth-century singers employ? If, as is not impossible, they sang with a nasal tone, ought we to do the same in a present-day performance or should we aim at producing a sound that is pleasing to listeners? Problems of this kind have to be faced, in a greater or lesser degree, in all music of the past.

Example 1(a)

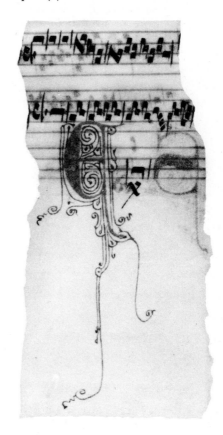

(b)

Ex-

[-iit sermo...]

A particular problem is associated with what is generally called troubadour or trouvère song. *Example 2* gives the original notation of one of these songs (from a Paris manuscript) and a possible transcription.

It will be noticed that the song includes not only groups of notes but also single notes: there is nothing, however, to show what relationship these notes bear to each other. The text here, unlike plainsong, is in verse, which means that some sort of rhythmical interpretation is possible. The transcription given above provides a consistent rhythm throughout the piece and accommodates the groups of notes in such a way that they fall comfortably into place. But it cannot, in the nature of things, have any final authority and certainly it should not be taken to imply that the rhythm suggested should be rigid. Song, more than any other form of music, calls for those fluctuations of rhythm mentioned earlier. A singer at the present day might well find it useful to use the transcription as a working basis for performance; but he would be well advised to sing it with a good deal of freedom.

Example 2(a)

*   *   *

In music as remote from our own time as this it is quite impossible to know what the

(*b*)

conventions of performance were. In later centuries, however, both theorists and composers offer us a good deal of information about methods of performance which are not immediately evident from the written notes. This is particularly true of rhythm in French music of the seventeenth and eighteenth centuries. As François Couperin said in his *L'Art de toucher le clavecin* (The art of playing the harpsichord, 1716), 'what we write is different from what we play'. A series of notes of apparently equal value would be modified in performance in such a way that the even-numbered notes would be shortened, with a consequent lengthening of the odd-numbered ones, or *vice versa*. The effect would be that the notes would now be unequal (*notes inégales*). It might happen, however, that a composer would want equal notes in a particular passage, in which case he would often specify *notes égales*, as in *Example 3*, as a warning against applying the usual convention of inequality. The direction *coulées* here means flowing:

be expressed exactly in precise, mathematical terms: it is for the performer to feel instinctively how much variation of the written notes would be appropriate in a particular passage or at a particular speed.

It is important to remember that inequality of this kind is a convention of French music. It would obviously be effective in music of other countries which is unmistakably written in the French style; but to apply it indiscriminately to all music of the seventeenth and eighteenth centuries shows a failure to realize that there was a difference in national styles and that there was no universal practice in operation throughout Europe. Another characteristically French convention was the lengthening, in certain circumstances, of dotted notes and the consequent shortening of the notes that followed. Among the writers who deal with this question is Johann Joachim Quantz in his manual on playing the flute, *Versuch einer Anweisung die Flöte traversiere zu spielen* (1752). He makes it clear that dotted minims and dotted crotchets

Example 3

It might be asked why composers, expecting inequality, did not indicate it in their notation – why, in fact, they did not write exactly what they wanted to be played. The answer is that this kind of inequality cannot

should have their normal length, but that when a note of smaller value is dotted it should be lengthened. *Example 4* on the following page gives his illustration of how this is to be done.

Example 4

(a)

(b)

The notes written underneath the interpretation are meant to show exactly how long the dotted quaver should last: the semiquaver of the original has become a hemidemisemiquaver, one quarter of its written value. Once again we should not take the demonstration too seriously as an exact representation of what is to be played: it is sufficient to note that the semiquaver should be short and precise and the dotted quaver correspondingly longer.

One very widespread convention at this period can be seen in *Example 5*, from Handel's *Messiah*, where (b) represents the correct performance of the opening bars.

It is particularly interesting to note that Handel has written the correct notation in bar 3. The reason for this is not carelessness or mere inconsistency on his part. The explanation is to be found in his autograph score. The initial semiquaver in bar 3 originally followed a dotted quaver. When he remodelled the opening of the recitative he deleted the earlier part of the bar as far as the semiquaver, replacing the deleted notes with rests: it was simpler to leave the semiquaver as it was rather than rewrite the bar in accordance with the accepted convention. We can be quite certain that the apparent inconsistency would not have worried Handel's players, who were used to playing (a) as (b). The convention was obviously a time-saving device: it takes less time to write a quaver rest followed by a quaver than a quaver rest plus a semiquaver rest followed by a semiquaver.

(b)

Example 5

Violino I

Violino II

Viola

Basso

Thus saith the Lord,

Bassi

the Lord of Hosts;   Yet once,a lit-tle while,   and I will

A particularly interesting example of the way in which short notes were played shorter than their notation is afforded by two versions of a keyboard overture by J. S. Bach: (*a*) is his original version in C minor; (*b*) is the version in B minor which he published in Part II of his *Clavier-Übung* in 1735. The semiquavers of the first version have become demisemiquavers in the second, which means that they were meant to be played as demisemiquavers (or a near approximation). It is interesting to note that Bach took particular pains to be perfectly clear about this when issuing his work to the public. He may very well have felt that not everyone would be as familiar with French practice as he was.

Example 6

(*a*)

(*b*)

A particular problem of eighteenth-century music which often worries performers today is concerned with accommodating three notes in one part with two in another. The problem is not made easier by the fact that Quantz and C. P. E. Bach do not agree about it, nor indeed do modern scholars. However, C. P. E. Bach's explanation (*Example 7*), which is supported by other evidence, seems a commonsense way of dealing with the question:

Example 7

The example means that when two notes are heard at the same time as three the second of the two should coincide with the third of the three. One result of this is that the treatment of a dotted note in this case is the reverse of what was illustrated in *Example 4*; here it is shorter, not longer, than the notation would suggest. C. P. E. Bach's example comes from the first part of his treatise on playing keyboard instruments, *Versuch über die wahre Art, das Clavier zu spielen*. This was originally published in 1753, three years after his father's death. It would obviously be a mistake to assume, as has sometimes been done, that everything he recommends applies to the performance of his father's work. However, the evidence of J. S. Bach's music strongly suggests that the same treatment of two against three is to be observed there. A familiar example is the chorale setting known in England as 'Jesu, joy of man's desiring', where the easy flow of the triplets played by the first violins and oboe would be seriously disturbed by a jerky rhythm in the lower parts. Even more convincing is the opening of the last movement of the fifth Brandenburg concerto (*Example 7*).

When the harpsichord enters the semiquavers must obviously coincide with the last notes of the triplets: it follows that the initial entry of the violin must be treated in the same way, i.e. it must be played ♪. Here again we have an example of a notation which was adopted in order to save time, and also to ensure clarity. It is quicker to write ♪ than ♪ and it is also clearer to the eye. Composers of Bach's time would not have bothered to explain this, since they were writing for performers who were thoroughly familiar with the convention.

* * *

Example 8

Another convention of the period which is not always understood at the present day occurs in recitative. Very few eighteenth-century writers refer to it. One of the few who do is Johann Friedrich Agricola in his *Anleitung zur Singkunst* (Introduction to the art of singing, 1757). This is a much enlarged German version of Pier Francesco Tosi's *Opinioni de' cantori antichi, e moderni o sieno osservazioni sopra il canto figurato* (1723), of which an English translation was published in 1742 under the title *Observations on the Florid Song, or Sentiments of the Ancient and Modern Singers*. Tosi speaks of recitative only in general terms, and his work does not include any music examples. Agricola augments the text considerably with comments of his own and offers illustrations of detailed points. *Example 9* on the following page shows two of those referring to the cadence.

Example 9

(a) illustrates the convention that where the voice drops a fourth (here from D to A) on to the final note or notes the drop is delayed. In (c) the voice drops a third (from D to B♭), and here the interval must be filled with the intermediate note (C). It will be noticed that in (a) the penultimate note of the accompaniment coincides with the singer's last two syllables ('–mo–re'). This is how accompaniments were normally written in the early eighteenth century. There is a widespread belief at the present day that the accompanist should wait until the singer has finished before playing his last two chords, but it is by no means certain that this was the universal practice at the time. Johann David Heinichen, in his *Der General-Bass in der Composition* (1728), emphasizes that in opera the accompanist should not wait, since this would be tiresome to listen to if it occurred frequently and would hold up the progress of the action. Georg Philipp Telemann, in his *Singe-, Spiel- und Generalbass-Übungen* (1733–5) makes a distinction between opera and cantatas: in opera the accompanist does not wait, in cantatas he generally does. It might be added that in recitatives accompanied by the orchestra it is often quite impossible to make a break before the final cadence without creating a ludicrous hiatus. The question naturally arises: how is the penultimate note of the accompaniment to be harmonized? (b) in *Example 9* is an editorial solution of this problem. The harmonic progression, with D

The singing master   *Richard Earlom after Godfried Schalcken c. 1680*

falling to C♯ in the player's right hand, is a conventional one at this period and fits smoothly with the singer's interpretation of his final syllables.

There is a further point about recitative which is made by Tosi and amplified by Agricola. Tosi emphasizes that church recitative is not to be sung in strict time. Agricola goes further and insists that this is true of all recitative. Naturally this does not apply to passages which have an accompaniment in regular rhythm played by several instruments, for instance the sections in Bach's *St. Matthew Passion* which are called recitative but, having a rhythmical accompaniment, would be more accurately described as *ariosi* (e.g. No. 60, '*Erbarm es Gott!*'). Elsewhere complete freedom is essential if the performance is not to become stiff and mechanical. The note-values written by the composer are a guide to the relative length of the syllables, nothing more. This is very often not understood by singers at the present day, who tend to sing all recitative at the same speed and at something very nearly approaching strict time. Conductors who insist on conducting recitative fall into the same error. A beat is necessary if the orchestra is accompanying, but it must be flexible and must follow what the singer is doing. Where the accompaniment is played only by a keyboard instrument and a cello or bass viol no direction from above is necessary: the accompanists simply follow the singer.

Continuo accompaniment

This brings us to the general question of keyboard accompaniment from a figured bass – an indispensable element in the performance of music of the seventeenth and eighteenth centuries. The figures (including accidentals), written either above or below the bass line, are a kind of musical shorthand, designed to save the composer time and to allow the keyboard-player a certain amount of freedom. The interpretation of the figures is simple. Thus the figure *3* means that the chord to be played includes a third above the bass: whether it is a major third or a minor third depends on the key. If the key is C major the accompanist will play E above a bass C; if it is C minor he will play E♭. Other intervals are interpreted in the same way. If a chord has to include a note which is not in the key this is indicated by the use of accidentals. Thus the sign ♯ above a bass E

means that G♯ must be played, not G♮: it is customary in this case to omit the figure *3*. With other intervals modified by flats or sharps the figure must be included. Thus *7♯* above a bass D means C♯, *6♭* above the same bass means B♭, and so on. The intervals may be played wherever it is convenient or appropriate. The normal practice was to play chords in the right hand and the bass only in the left. This means, for example, that E above C would not be the E in the middle of the bass stave but the E on the first line of the treble stave, or even an octave above that.

The system came into general use in the seventeenth century as an ideal way of supplying an inconspicuous accompaniment to a solo singer, but it was found to be equally useful in instrumental music. In the early years figures were sparsely used, and the accompanist often had to keep his eye on the solo line to see what chords would be appropriate. But it was soon found necessary to give more precise directions, though cases occur where a bass is not figured at all, either because the composer was too lazy or because he was going to play the accompaniment

Rehearsal of a cantata

himself, or possibly because the figures were not entered in the score but only in the bass part (the *basso continuo*), which has disappeared. Though the system was designed originally for accompanying a soloist it proved equally useful for accompanying a group of voices or instruments or indeed any kind of ensemble (see *Example 3*). In a large ensemble it may not always be easy to hear a keyboard instrument, but as C. P. E. Bach pointed out you notice if it is not there.

Since one of the principal functions of the figured bass in the early seventeenth century – for instance, in the operas of Peri, Caccini and Monteverdi – was to accompany recitative, which was not sung in strict time, it follows that any accompaniment had to be of the simplest possible kind. This principle is often disregarded in performances of this music at the present day, either through a lack of confidence in the singers or because it is felt that a plain texture needs somehow to be animated and elaborated. One of the arguments in favour of elaboration is based on a misinterpretation of an early treatise on continuo-playing, Agostino Agazzari's *Del sonare sopra'l basso con tutti li stromenti e dell'uso*

loro nel conserto (On playing above the bass with all the instruments and their use in consort, 1607). As the title implies, Agazzari was not writing solely for keyboard-players. He divides the instruments he is discussing into two categories: (1) what he calls 'foundation instruments', i.e. those capable of playing chords, such as the harpsichord, lute and harp; (2) 'ornamental instruments', those which play melodic lines, including the lute when used for this purpose. The foundation instruments are there to give a firm support: they must not under any circumstances interfere with the voice or voices that they are accompanying. The ornamental instruments can indulge in various kinds of elaboration; but Agazzari gives no example of what he means, and there is nothing in his little work to suggest that the ornamental instruments are to be used to accompany a solo voice. The only example of filling up a bass line which he gives is designed for a keyboard instrument, probably the organ. It is shown in *Example 10* together with a transcription into modern notation. (The chord marked with an asterisk has had a note corrected from G to A.)

Example 10(a)

This is very simple and gives no support to any theory that the accompanist to a singer in the early seventeenth century indulged in flights of fancy.

It is obvious that where the music is in a regular rhythm the accompanist has more opportunity to make a personal contribution. But here too it remains an inflexible rule that he must not under any circumstances distract attention from the principal part or parts: his role is purely subsidiary. It is on record that J. S. Bach showed, as one might expect, remarkable ingenuity in transforming a figured bass into something that had a life of its own. According to his son, C. P. E. Bach, he would on occasion accompany a trio in such a way that by adding a new melodic part he converted it into a quartet. While his contemporaries naturally were lost in amazement at this virtuosity there is no need to suppose that we should take this written testimony as a criterion for accompanying Bach's own music, or any other music of the same period. We have, after all, no examples of this prodigious invention that we can study, which is understandable since it was exercised on the spur of the moment. The only solid evidence we posess for harmonizing Bach's basses is a continuo part which he wrote out himself, presumably for a pupil. The passage in question comes from a bass aria in his Cantata No. 3, *Ach Gott, wie manches Herzeleid*, for the second Sunday after Epiphany (1725). *Example 11* shows first the introduction to the aria from the original score of the cantata, where it is in F♯ minor, followed by a written-out accompaniment transposed to E minor. The important thing to notice here is that the original bass line has a strong melodic character of its own, which would be obscured if any attempt were made to introduce any other melodic interest above it. Bach's harmonization should not be dismissed as merely elementary instruction for an unskilled pupil: it should be studied as a model of good taste and musicianship, even though there are details in it that might not be approved by pedants.

Example 11

(a)

(b)

Playing from figured bass is still taught in universities, but expert practitioners are relatively few. For this reason editors of old music have for a long time supplied their own version (now quaintly described as a 'realization') of what the harpsichordist or the organist should play. These versions range from the misplaced ingenuity shown in some older vocal scores of Bach's cantatas to harmonizations so jejune and monotonous that they are more likely to send the player to sleep than to encourage him to take an active part in what is going on. For this reason a player who does not trust himself to play direct from the figured bass should write out his own part, either direct from the bass or from a modern editor's version, introducing such modifications as he thinks will be effective. There are many ways in which a plain accompaniment can be varied, particularly by the use of passing notes, without drawing attention to the player. Seventeenth and eighteenth-century musicians would have been horrified at some of the ways in which present-day continuo-players advertise their presence: singers and solo instrumentalists, in particular, would have objected strongly to any invasion of their territory. The cause of good taste is not advanced by critics who single out a continuo-player for praise because of some flight of fancy which has attracted their attention. Comic opera is a particularly dangerous area for accompanists. The temptation to underline the humour of a recitative with some quirk on the keyboard may be very strong but it ought to be resisted. The singer is the funny man, not the accompanist. Mozart may introduce humorous touches into the orchestral accompaniment of an aria; but it is very doubtful whether he would have sanctioned impromptu witticisms on the keyboard.

Ornamentation

Continuo accompaniment, however discreet, is a form of controlled improvisation. The player is tied to the bass and to the

Title page from *Lexikon* by J. G. Walther published in 1732

prescribed harmony, but within these limits he is free to interpret his part in any way that is appropriate to the style of the music, the forces engaged and the building in which the performance is taking place. Improvisation also has a part to play in another area of the music of this period: ornamentation. Ornamentation may be (1) indicated by conventional signs; (2) written out in full; (3) left entirely to the performer. A good deal of the music of this period which appears to the eye to have almost a virginal purity was ornamented as a matter of course in performance. This applies not only to solo music but also to music for an ensemble. We know

The concert   *Lorenzo Costa*, c. 1488

that sixteenth and early seventeenth century madrigals were decorated in performance, and church music could be treated in the same way. This is clear from a handbook published by Giovanni Battista Bovicelli in 1594 under the title *Regole, Passaggi di musica*, with the sub-title *Madrigali, e motetti passeggiati*. *Passaggi* here means ornamental treatment of simple melodic lines. Bovicelli, who was a singer in the choir of Milan Cathedral, begins with preliminary studies, designed to show how a simple sequence of notes could be ornamented. He then proceeds to print the soprano line of a number of compositions and

to place underneath it the ornamentation which he recommends. *Example 12* shows the beginning of what appears to be a motet by Palestrina – a setting of the text *Ave verum corpus*. In fact this is an adaptation of sacred words to one of Palestrina's madrigals.

The clef at the beginning is the C clef on the first line, corresponding to middle C on the piano. The vertical line after the barred C of the time-signature is a rest, with the duration of two breves. It stands here because the soprano enters after other parts. Palestrina's original begins on A, and Bovicelli's ornamented version on F.

Example 12(a)

Bovicelli points out that he has chosen well-known works so that people who use his book can try out the effect of combining his version of the soprano with the other voices. It would, in any case, be impossible to ornament the other voices in the same way; the result would be confusion. But it is not impossible that discreet ornamentation of parts other than the soprano could be introduced in cadences, provided that every singer knew what the others were doing.

The ability to improvise ornaments was an indispensable part of the equipment of any singer at this time and later. A contribution towards the study of this art was made by Giovanni Luca Conforto, a singer in the papal choir at Rome, who published (apparently in 1593) a little book entitled *Breve e facile maniera di essercitarsi ad ogni scolaro non solamente a far passagi sopra tutte le note . . . ma ancora per poter da se senza maestri scrivere ogni opera et aria passeggiata*. The wordy title simply means that the book is designed to teach

students to ornament and also to write ornamented music without instruction. *Example 13* shows seven ways how to ornament a cadence. (*b*) shows a modern transcription.

The simple cadence comes at the beginning: it consists of the notes B A G A. G should, of course, be G♯ as it is the leading note and needs to be a semitone below A. It would automatically have been sung as such. In the various ornamented cadences which follow, the sharp (rather a scratchy sign) is marked where it occurs. F should also be sharp in the second, third, fourth and seventh versions. The singing of sharps and flats where they are not marked was part of the tradition of *musica ficta* (false music). The tradition goes back to the time when all music was, at least theoretically, based on the modes, which correspond to scales on the white notes of the piano, beginning respectively on D, E, F and G. *Musica ficta* meant that you pretended that you were observing the mode while inserting sharps and flats at appropriate places

Example 13(a)

in the interests of a smooth melodic progression or a convincing harmonic cadence. It was not until the seventeenth century that composers and copyists accepted the inevitable fact that accidentals would be introduced in certain places and so wrote them into the music to avoid misunderstanding. Until then there was no sort of consistency in the writing of accidentals; sometimes they were left out where they were certainly needed, sometimes they were inserted where they were in any case obvious. This is more a problem for editors than for performers, who do not normally use original sources. But in a sense editors are also interpreters. They are reliable interpreters if they make a clear distinction between what is in the original and what they have added. If they fail to do this, they are wolves in sheep's clothing and should be distrusted.

* * *

Fully written-out ornamentation is comparatively rare in the seventeenth century, for the very good reason that it tended to cramp the imagination and skill of performers. There is an unusual example in Monteverdi's opera *Orfeo* (1607), which may be regarded as a parallel to the kind of ornamentation provided by Bovicelli. It occurs at a supreme moment in the opera, when Orpheus, having descended to Hades in search of Eurydice, appeals to Charon to ferry him across the River Styx. To persuade the ferryman he needs all his legendary skill as a singer, and hence embarks on an extremely elaborate recitative, in which instruments also play an important part. The curious thing is that the printed score, published in 1609, includes both a plain version of the recitative and an ornamented version of it. See *example 14* (*a*) on page 26.

The direction at the top of the page says: 'Orpheus, to the sound of the organ and a *chitarrone* (a large lute), sings one only of the two parts'. (*a*) is the opening of the scene as it appears in the original score; (*b*) is a transcription into modern notation, which shows more clearly how the two violins follow each other. The repeated notes which occur in the ornamented voice-part in the second, fourth and fifth bars are a kind of *vibrato*, which was known at the time as the *trillo* (what we call a trill was known then as a *gruppo*). The proper execution of the *trillo* was an essential part of a singer's technique. In a letter of 1610 to the Duke of Mantua, Monteverdi reports on a singer who came for an audition with a view to employment at the ducal court. Among his favourable comments is the observation: '*Ha trillo assai bono*' (he has a very good *trillo*).

Example 14(a)

We may reasonably assume that the ornamentation written out in *Orfeo* is the work of the composer. In other cases where such ornamentation is provided we may have to suspend judgment; but in so far as it is contemporary it can be accepted as giving a fair picture of what would have been expected of a performer at the time. About 1711 the London publisher John Walsh issued an edition of Corelli's violin sonatas with the following title:

*XII Sonata's or Solo's for a Violin a Bass Violin
or Harpsicord
Compos'd by Arcangelo Corelli.
His fifth Opera* [i.e. Op. 5].
*This Edition has yᵉ advantage of haveing
yᵉ Graces to all yᵉ Adagio's and other
places where the Author thought proper*

(A previous edition had been published at Amsterdam, with 'graces' for the slow movements of only the first six sonatas). *Example 15* shows the beginning of the first movement of the second sonata as it appears in Walsh's edition.

If we assume that the text of this edition was published with Corelli's authority (he died in 1713), it is perhaps significant that only the slow movements are ornamented. We know, however, that other violinists of the time played the quick movements as well with ornamentation, sometimes of an extravagant kind. This is not on the whole a case where a present-day performer, anxious to show his understanding of past practice, would be advised to imitate his predecessors. Ornamentation of a slow movement can give life and colour to a simple melody and enhance the expression. In a quick movement it can easily disturb the melodic outline, not to mention the rhythm, and may serve only to demonstrate the player's virtuosity. It is not surprising that some composers of the seventeenth and eighteenth centuries expressed disapproval of improvised ornamentation and insisted that singers and players

should perform what was written; though, as Giovanni Maria Bononcini pointed out in 1672, this does not apply to 'certain graces, which . . . when well employed ornament and add beauty to the compositions'. In other words, good taste, which is easier to prescribe than to define, is the criterion.

*   *   *

The indication of ornaments by conventional signs was common throughout Europe but was particularly thorough and precise in French music and in music written in the French style in other countries. Not only theorists but also composers gave detailed directions for the interpretation of these ornaments, and these directions are of great value to the modern interpreter even though the authors are not always in complete agreement. The importance of ornaments was stressed by François Couperin in the preface to his third book of harpsichord pieces, published in 1722. He expressed his surprise that, in spite of the fact that he had carefully marked all the ornaments in his pieces, there were people who did not take the trouble to observe them. '*C'est une négligence*', he wrote, with some heat, '*qui n'est pas pardonnable*': the introduction of ornaments was not in his view a matter for individual choice:

Je déclare que mes pièces doivent être exécutées comme je les ai marquées et qu'elles ne feront jamais impression sur les personnes qui ont le goût vrai, tant qu'on n'observera pas à la lettre tout ce que j'ai marqué, sans augmentation ni diminution.

(I declare that my pieces must be performed as I have marked them, and that they will never make an impression on people who have true taste, so long as everything I have marked is not scrupulously observed, without any addition or subtraction.)

The number of signs used for ornaments in the seventeenth and eighteenth centuries is bewildering in its complexity, and this is not the place to discuss them in detail.

Example 15

One of the shortest tables of ornaments is the one which J. S. Bach provided for the instruction of his son Wilhelm Friedemann in 1720. *Example 16* gives the original and a translation into modern notation:

The heading reads: 'Explanation of various signs, showing how to play certain graces nicely'. The *trillo* has its modern meaning of 'trill' or 'shake': it will be noticed that it begins on a note above the principal note and

Example 16(a)

(b)

Explication unterschiedlicher Zeichen, so gewiße *manieren* artig zu spielen, andeuten.

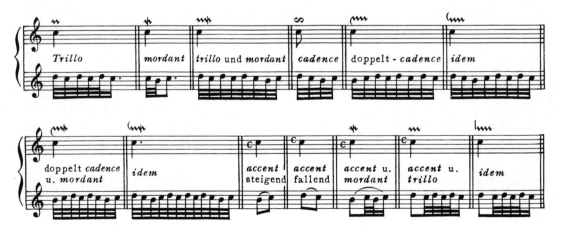

does not continue throughout. The *mordant* (or 'mordent', as it is generally spelt in English) is, as its name implies, an ornament with a bite and is played very crisply. The *cadence* is what we should call a 'turn', beginning on a note above the principal note. The curved signs at the beginning of the next two ornaments show that one approaches the trill respectively from below or from above. The *accent*, whether rising from below (*steigend*) or falling from above (*fallend*), is what is now known as 'appoggiatura' (literally 'a leaning'). The combined ornaments in the table do not call for comment. It is clearly valuable to have the authority of so distinguished a composer for the interpretation of these ornaments and one cannot help feeling grateful that it is so concise. At the same time it must be admitted that it does not cover all the ornaments to be found in Bach's own works, and in some respects it does not offer sufficient information. This is particularly true of the *accent* or appoggiatura, which merely shows what happens when the sign precedes a crotchet. This question, which has given rise to a good deal of conjecture and

arbitrary definition, will be dealt with a little later.

Bach, like his contemporaries, used signs for ornaments extensively, but there are many places, and even complete pieces, where they are omitted in accordance with the accepted principle that experienced performers would know where to add them. We have, however, one particularly interesting example of the kind of ornamentation that Bach would have expected in a piece where none was marked. No. 5 of his *sinfonie* for the keyboard (often referred to as 'three-part inventions') was originally written without ornaments: these were added later. *Example 17* overleaf, shows the opening of both versions, one plain the other ornamented.

The small notes, slurred to the main note following, are another form of the *accent* or appoggiatura. Reference to Bach's table of ornaments will show how to interpret those that are found here but will not help to determine how long the appoggiaturas should be. A study of the ornamented version of this piece should serve as a useful guide to any keyboard-player who is enterprising enough

Title page from *Psalmodia Christiana* by Hector Mithobius, published in 1665

Example 17

(a)

to introduce ornaments into other pieces where few or none are marked. It should be remembered that Bach did not publish his *Inventionen* and *sinfonie* and therefore, unlike Couperin, had no need to give complete and detailed instructions to performers.

Bach not only used signs for ornaments. He also, on occasion, wrote out ornamentation in full, for instance in his works for violin solo and notably in the first two sonatas. As with the ornamentation attributed to Corelli the ornamentation is found in the slow movements, where it would make the maximum effect. *Example 18*, opposite, is the opening of the first movement of Sonata No. 1. (The indication *tr* means the same as the first of the signs in *Example 16*). It would be comparatively easy, but quite profitless, to reduce this to a simple melodic line, in which case it would be similar to dozens of slow movements of the period which on paper appear to make a virtue of simplicity.

Example 18

(continued)

*   *   *

The previous examples (*Examples 15–18*) have all dealt with instrumental music. Similar principles, however, were applied to vocal music but not, in the eighteenth century, to recitative, which by this time had become mainly a connecting link between arias: its principal function was to bear the brunt of a narrative or to provide a vehicle for conversation. Ornamentation would have been inappropriate in what was virtually the equivalent of speech. In the aria, however, there was plenty of opportunity for display over and above what the composer had provided – particularly in the *da capo* aria, where the first section of a three-part structure was repeated after the contrast provided by a middle section (*da capo* means 'from the beginning'). The normal practice was to sing the first time more or less what the composer wrote and then on the return of this section to add 'graces'. How far this was feasible depended naturally on the character of the music. As in a quick instrumental movement, an aria which included a good deal of elaborate and rapid figuration would leave little opportunity for additions by the singer. It was rather in the more tranquil pieces that singers had an opportunity to display not only their technique but their imagination. Naturally enough, relatively few examples survive of such methods, simply because they

were improvised at the time and there was no means of recording them. *Example 19*, from Handel's *Messiah*, will give some idea of what an eighteenth-century singer might have done with 'I know that my Redeemer liveth'. (*a*) is Handel's original text, (*b*) is a version found in a manuscript which formerly belonged to Jenny Lind's husband, Otto Goldschmidt, and before that to the eighteenth-century conductor William Hayes.

This treatment of what appears to be a simple and dignified melodic line may very well shock people who have been accustomed to hearing a more recent tradition of oratorio performances; and this raises the whole question of how far it is either possible or desirable to attempt an 'authentic' interpretation, to which we shall return later. It is worth noting here, however, that there is no evidence that the 'Goldschmidt' version is what Handel himself wanted, though he probably expected his singers to improvise some ornamentation of the vocal line. The operative word here is 'improvise'. A performance in which a singer obediently performs an ornamented version provided by a modern editor or conductor will certainly not be giving us what Handel wanted. Ornamentation must spring from the singer's own instinct for what is effective and beautiful and from an understanding of what the apparently plain original implies.

It will be remembered that Bach's table of ornaments (*Example 16*) includes a simple

Example 19

(a)

I know that — my Re — deem — er liv — eth

(b)

I know that —— my Re - deem - er liv - eth

explanation of the *accent* or appoggiatura – a division of a crotchet into two quavers. This is clear enough, but it does not provide an answer to all the places in Bach's works where an appoggiatura is marked. In consequence editors and others have turned to the theoretical works of Quantz and C. P. E. Bach. Quantz was writing primarily about playing the flute, and C. P. E. Bach about playing the harpsichord, clavichord or piano; but there is no reason to suppose that they would not have applied their recommendations to other instruments and to singing. Some of Quantz's examples are given in *example 20*.

Though he uses a small quaver as the sign for the appoggiatura (which he calls *Vorschlag*)

it is obvious from the examples that the value of the note has no precise significance. According to the circumstances it can take half or two-thirds or three-fifths of the note to which it is prefixed. What appears to be the principal note therefore becomes subordinate, so far as its length is concerned. But Johann Mattheson, in his encyclopedic *Der vollkommene Capellmeister* (The complete musical director, 1739), emphasizes that the appoggiatura must be performed so smoothly that the two notes seem to melt into one; and since the principal note is part of the harmony and the appoggiatura is not, it still remains the more important of the two, however much it may be shortened. It might be asked why composers should use miniature

Example 20

(a) (written)   (performed)

(b)

(c)

symbols for the appoggiatura instead of writing exactly what they wanted to be played or sung. The answer is to be found partly in a traditional theory of harmony. The appoggiatura is not strictly a part of the chord over which it is heard and is therefore presented, so to speak, apologetically as an ornament to the harmony. An additional reason is that, in spite of Quantz's precise interpretations, the actual length of the appoggiatura was something to be decided by the performer's taste and could not therefore be exactly represented in conventional notation.

This, however, did not prevent C. P. E. Bach, like many other theorists, from giving equally precise instructions. His examples (*Example 21*), which use notes of different value for different appoggiaturas, go even further than Quantz's in reducing the length of the principal note and even, in some cases, push it into the place of a rest, which then disappears.

Attempts have been made to apply the recommendations of Quantz and C. P. E. Bach to the works of J. S. Bach. The grounds for doing this, however, are not very substantial. Quantz's book was published in 1752, two years after Bach's death, and though it is the fruit of many years professional experience it is clearly concerned with a more elegant and more fashionable type of music than Bach's. The same is true of C. P. E. Bach's work, the first part of which originally appeared in 1753. To use his recommendations as a literal guide to the interpretation of his father's works is not only unreasonable but may easily lead to gross distortions. The only possible way of interpreting Bach's works is to start with the simple table given in *Example 16* and to study also all the places where the composer has written out ornaments, including appoggiaturas. This method, which must be controlled by good taste, is far more likely to achieve artistic results than arbitrary judgments based on what eighteenth-century theorists wrote. Reliance on theory is in fact one of the dangers of over-zealous scholarship. Not all theorists of the past agreed with each other, nor were methods of interpretation stereotyped throughout Europe or indeed within a single country.

There is an interesting letter in which Haydn gives detailed instructions about the performance of one of his own works. He had written a Latin cantata in 1768 for the jubilee of the abbot of a Cistercian monastery. As he could not be present when the work was performed he wrote to say what he wanted done. One of his points concerns the appoggiatura. *Example 22* shows first the written text of his

Example 21

example (almost as it appears in the cantata) and secondly not only how it was to be sung, but how it was not to be sung:

Example 22

(a)

quae me - ta - mor - pho - sis

(b)

quae me - ta - mor - pho - sis

not

quae me - ta - mor - pho - sis

We have here a rare eighteenth-century example of a composer giving not merely general advice on interpretation but precise instructions about a particular passage. It follows that all the appoggiaturas in Haydn's cantata, and presumably in his other works (at least of this period), should be interpreted in the same way.

Rhythm

Our examples have been drawn mainly from the seventeenth and eighteenth centuries, since there is a good deal of written evidence from this period to show either how music was performed or how authoritative writers thought it should be performed. It was important also to spend some time on these examples, since the music is sufficiently distant from our own time to have left no reliable tradition of performance. But even nearer the twentieth century there have been conventions which have been widely observed but not represented by notation or even documented by writers. Variations of tempo or rhythm are part of the life-blood of music; but in the past they were not indicated by composers, and even when such indications came into use, they could not in the nature of things be precise. The instructions which Frescobaldi printed in the preface to his first book of keyboard toccatas (1614) were quite unusual for the period:

Prèmieramente, che non deve questo modo di sonare stare soggetto à battuta; come veggiamo usarsi ne i Madrigali moderni, i quali quantunque difficili si agevolano per mezzo della battuta portandola hor languida hor veloce, è sostenendola etiando in aria, secondo i loro affetti, o senso delle parole.

(First of all, this method of playing must not be governed by the beat. We can see the same thing in the modern madrigals, which, however difficult they are, are made easier by fluctuations of the beat from slow to quick or even by holding up the rhythm [i.e. with a pause] according to the emotions expressed or the meaning of the words.)

This is valuable, not only as a guide to Frescobaldi's music but as a pointer towards an intelligent interpretation of early seventeenth-century madrigals.

That players in the eighteenth century varied the rhythm is evident from what C. P. E. Bach says on the subject, and also from a letter which Mozart wrote to his father in October 1777:

Everyone is amazed that I can always keep strict time. What these people cannot grasp is that in *tempo rubato* in an Adagio the left hand should go on playing in strict time.

This is a different kind of fluctuation. *Tempo rubato* means literally 'robbed time'; but Mozart lays down the principle that what is robbed has to be paid back – the fluctuation is in the melody, not in the accompaniment. A Norwegian pupil of Chopin's, Thomas Tellefsen, recalled that he was criticized by his teacher when he said he was playing *rubato*. Chopin said he was doing nothing of the kind: he was playing out of time. To illustrate his own conception of *rubato* he blew gently on a candle flame: to illustrate Tellefsen's he blew the candle out. The anecdote is illuminating and reinforces the principle that nuances which are implied but not stated in music need to be treated with circumspection: only it takes a genuine artist to see what the implications are. Style is something that cannot be grasped by a rough and ready acquaintance. One needs to soak oneself in the music of any composer, or any period, before one is really at home with it.

Style

The Germans, who like compound words, have coined the term *Aufführungspraxis*, which merely means the way people sang and played. They do not normally apply it to music later than the eighteenth century, though, in fact, the nineteenth century had its conventions too. One way to learn something of these conventions might be to listen to piano rolls played by composers, if it were not that these records from the past on the whole strengthen the view that composers are not the best interpreters of their own music. Something may be learned from early gramophone records, in spite of their technical imperfections. The evidence they offer may sometimes be disconcerting or even offensive to our ideas of what nineteenth-century music should sound like. Older people may recall how musicians brought up in the circle of Brahms and his contemporaries played Romantic music. A common mannerism of pianists was to avoid playing chords simultaneously in the right and left hands. Furtwängler is said to have aimed at a similar lack of precision in the orchestra. Traditions can sometimes be passed on from one generation to the next, but they easily evaporate as time goes on. Debussy as a small boy was taught the piano by Mme Mauté de Fleurville (mother-in-law of Verlaine), who had been a pupil of Chopin.

Violinist playing in the French style
Gerard Dou, 1665

Many years later he recalled what she told him about her teacher:

Chopin wanted his pupils to study without using the pedal and only to use it sparingly when performing. It was this use of the pedal as a kind of breathing that I noticed in Liszt, when I heard him in Rome.

Debussy himself as a student is said to have been a clumsy pianist; but in his maturity he was noted for the extreme delicacy of his playing. His biographer Léon Vallas says that he 'made one forget that the piano has hammers'.

String-playing has changed a good deal over the years. Until François Tourte perfected the modern bow in the late eighteenth century violinists used a bow in which the wood was slightly curved away from the hair. Anyone who has heard seventeenth- or early eighteenth-century music performed with a bow of this kind will remember that it makes possible a detached style of playing in which the articulation of individual notes makes for a vivid and strongly rhythmical performance.

Seventeenth - century composers did not always indicate consistently where two or more notes were to be taken in the same bow. In *Example 23,* from No. 9 of Purcell's

Example 23

(continued)

39

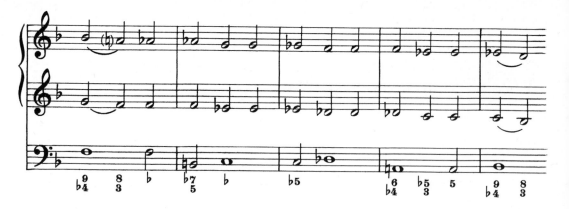

Sonatas of IV Parts, published after his death, probability suggests that the slurs marked in the opening part of the movement and elsewhere should be applied wherever there is a similar figuration, though naturally it is impossible to be absolutely sure.

Methods of bowing varied from one country to another. Corelli in Rome is said to have had difficulty in playing an overture as Handel wanted it. The composer, infuriated (so the story goes) by this lack of comprehension, snatched the violin from Corelli's hand and played the passage himself. Whereupon Corelli meekly explained: '*Ma, caro Sassone,*

The right and wrong way of playing the violin from the treatise by Leopold Mozart published in 1756

Example 24

(a) **Menuet**

(b)

questa Musica è nel stylo Francese, di ch'io non m'intendo' (But, dear Saxon, this music is in the French style, with which I am not familiar). Georg Muffat, who spent several years in Paris, devotes a substantial part of the introduction to his *Florilegium Secundum* (1698) to bowing methods. *Example 24*, from this work, shows a minuet bowed in two different ways, one (a) Italian and the other (b) French. The version given below Muffat's text shows the French bowing translated into modern symbols.

If we can believe that the Italian bowing is authentic the differences are striking. The Italian begins with an up-bow and simply alternates up and down throughout the piece. The French has a down-bow on the first beat of each bar, even though this twice involves having two down-bows in succession, and where necessary takes two notes in one bow. In view of Muffat's experience it is obviously sensible to take seriously his demonstration of French bowing, even if one has doubts about the Italian. Many modern editions of string music of the seventeenth and eighteenth centuries are marred by indiscriminate bowing, which ignores the style of the music

and takes the life-blood out of it.

This does not mean that bowing should never be added. It certainly needs to be in Bach's works, where indications of bowing are often inconsistent, no doubt because once a pattern has been established players familiar with the style will automatically reproduce it throughout a movement. Bach's phrasing of wind parts shows a similar inconsistency. Nineteenth-century composers were generally more scrupulous, though Wagner, in particular, was liable to draw large slurs over passages for string instruments which could not possibly be played in one bow. One assumes that in such cases the leader of each section was expected to tell the others what to do, as he often does at the present day. However careful a composer he may be, and however experienced, his bowing may not be the best possible, though if he is a string-player himself one can expect it to be practical. From the late nineteenth century onwards most composers have been meticulous in indicating the bowing they want – and often more than the bowing. *Example 25*, on the following page, is the viola part from the opening of Elgar's *Dream of Gerontius*.

Example 25

Here not only is every detail of the bowing marked, with the appropriate dynamics, but fingering is indicated as well.

*   *   *

Fingering in keyboard music may be less helpful to the performer. Brahms's fingering of his piano works is highly idiosyncratic and seems to have been designed for his own use. On the other hand Chopin's fingering is often a clue to phrasing and expression, and the same is true, at an earlier period, of Couperin's. Though it is known that clear articulation (which does not mean *staccato*) was favoured in harpsichord and organ music in the seventeenth and eighteenth centuries, particularly in quick movements, this did not exclude the use of smooth phrasing in appropriate places. Bach's phrasing in his organ works, as in his music for other instruments, is on the whole sparse and not always consistent; but where it does occur its purpose is always obvious, and from such places one can tell by analogy where it should be introduced when it is not marked. Strictly speaking, a true *legato* is possible neither on the harpsichord nor on the piano, but it is possible to create the illusion. In the title of his two-part *Inventionen* Bach spoke of the necessity for cultivating a *cantabile* or singing style of playing, and other composers have made the same point. Schubert wrote to his father and stepmother in July 1825:

I produced my four-handed Variations and marches with notable success. What pleased especially were the variations in my new Sonata for two hands, which I performed alone and not without merit, since several people assured me that the keys become singing voices under my hands, which, if true, pleases me greatly, since I cannot endure the accursed chopping in which even distinguished pianoforte players indulge and which delights neither the ear nor the mind.

*   *   *

If styles of playing have changed, so have instruments – not always for the better. Even the violin, which has not altered its structure, has changed its tone by the use of metal, instead of gut, strings. There has been an increase in brilliance and a gain in reliability, but those who recall the days when gut strings were normal are likely to feel that something has been lost. The horn changed its character as soon as it was fitted with valves in the early nineteenth century, though players brought up on traditional lines were able to preserve its tone well into the twentieth century. But the demands of modern orchestral scores, and once again the urge for reliability, led to the addition of a further complex of tubing which marked a further departure from the mellow tones that our forefathers knew. The organ has gone through so many developments in the course of the years and in different countries that there is no such thing as a typical organ: the only thing common to all organs is the capacity to sustain sound indefinitely and to cover a wide range of dynamics, from very soft to very loud. As for the piano, it has changed so much that an instrument of Mozart's day sounds as if it belonged to a different family. Without subscribing to E. C. Bentley's malicious quatrain:

> The Abbé Liszt
> Hit the piano with his fist.
> That was the way
> He used to play,

one is bound to point out that the powerful style of piano-playing exploited by Liszt and his contemporaries led not only to the strengthening of the structure of the instrument but also to a considerable increase of sonority and a consequent lack of clarity. The bass of the modern piano is muddy compared with the instrument for which Mozart and Beethoven wrote, and the deeper touch makes it more difficult to produce effective trills. The thick chords in the left hand, to which Beethoven was addicted, are effective on an early nineteenth-century piano because the individual notes are clear.

Liszt at the piano

Tempo

The details of interpretation will differ according to the medium employed. But there are two basic problems which all interpreters must face: one is tempo, the other expression. Before the seventeenth century, composers did not indicate the speed at which they wished their music to be performed: the note-values which they used were supposed to be sufficient indication. In the sixteenth century the basic unit was the minim (once the shortest note, as its name implies), which moved at a moderate speed which cannot, for obvious reasons, be precisely defined. If a more lively movement was required, for instance in a light-hearted madrigal, notes of shorter value would be used within the framework of a time-system based on the minim. Alternatively, in triple time, a proportional sign would be used to indicate a substantial increase of speed: thus

J. Danhauser, 1840

the sign $\frac{3}{1}$ meant that a bar of three semibreves should take the time of a single semibreve in normal notation: this usage survived into the seventeenth century. The use of adjectives to indicate speed seems to have been adopted in the first instance for instrumental music; their application to vocal music was more gradual, presumably because in many cases the words would give a sufficiently clear indication of what the speed should be. The adjectives originated in Italy and spread over most of Europe, though the French, with characteristic independence, preferred to use their own language. Purcell used the Italian terms in his *Sonatas of III Parts* (1683) and he, or his publisher, explained them in the preface:

It remains only that the English Practitioner be enform'd, that he will find a few terms of Art perhaps unusual to him, the chief of which are these following: *Adagio* and *Grave*, which import nothing but a very slow movement: *Presto Largo*, *Poco Largo*, or *Largo* by itself, a middle movement: *Allegro*, and *Vivace*, a very brisk, swift, or fast movement: *Piano*, soft.

It might be argued that this description is not particularly helpful, since 'fast' and 'slow' are relative terms; but the same criticism might be made of the Italian words. *Adagio* properly means 'at ease', and *allegro* means 'lively'. It was this uncertainty that led to various attempts to define speed more exactly. Quantz, for instance, adopted as the unit the human pulse, which he took at 80 beats to the minute. This is naturally an arbitrary unit, since the human pulse varies according to age, sex, activity and so on. However, Quantz's 80 per minute provided a useful basis for calculating the speed of dance movements of his time, which in several cases seem to be a good deal faster than we should be inclined to take them today. At the same time experiments were going on to use a pendulum as a more accurate basis on which to work. The final stage of these experiments came when Johann Nepomuk Maelzel in the early nineteenth century patented his metronome, which enabled one to adjust the speed to various fractions of a minute:

thus, $\unicode{x2669} = 60$ means that each crotchet lasts exactly one second, $\unicode{x2669} = 120$ means that there are two crotchets per second. This instrument made a strong impression on Beethoven, who used it to indicate the speed of a number of his compositions. These speeds have sometimes been challenged, partly on the ground that he was deaf, and partly because it is alleged that his metronome was defective.

As a starting-point for determining the speed of a piece a metronome is obviously useful; but it can be misleading, for the very good reason that it is a machine and human beings are not. However precise the metronomic indications that a composer adds to his music, they do not necessarily tell us exactly what was in his mind. He may, for example, have decided on the speed of an orchestral work when playing it over on the piano, without realizing that it would sound very different when it came to performance in a large hall. Some composers, in fact, have changed their minds about speed after an experience of this kind, and quite a number do not necessarily follow their own markings when performing. The metronome, however, can be useful in inculcating a sense of absolute speed, which can be as valuable to a musician as a sense of absolute pitch. A man who can beat 60 or 80 or 120 beats to the minute will be able to approximate very closely to a speed indicated by a metronome mark and will find it easier to move from one tempo to another.

Some composers at the present day leave the performer a little liberty by writing, for example, $\unicode{x2669} = 80\text{–}90$; others do not use metronome marks at all, or if they do, leave some doubt about changes in speed, writing *poco meno mosso* (a little slower), for instance, without saying how much slower than the metronomic speed previously indicated. At the other extreme are composers like Bartók, who indicates the exact length of time that each section of a movement is to take, as well as the length of the complete movement. Thus in the first movement of his fifth string quartet the first 13 bars are supposed to take $24\frac{1}{2}$ seconds, the next 11 bars 22 seconds, and so on. But whether the indications are precise or vague the performer still has to make up his own mind about the speed which he is going to adopt, and this is clearly imperative in music written before the invention of the metronome, where it is necessary to decide what the composer meant by *allegro* or *andante* or *adagio*. Even if a decision is reached on this point it will still be subject to modification according to the size of the building in which the performance is taking place and its resonance or lack of it.

*   *   *

The Italian terms used to indicate speed have changed their meaning in the course of time. *Adagio* (literally 'at ease', 'leisurely') already meant 'very slow', as we have seen, in Purcell's time. On the other hand, *largo* (literally 'broad') meant 'a middle movement', i.e. the equivalent of the later *moderato*, though later composers interpreted it as 'slow'. *Andante* means properly 'going', 'walking', but it came to be used as the tempo mark for a moderately slow movement. *Andantino*, a diminutive of *andante*, is obviously an ambiguous term: does it mean a little slower than *andante* or a little faster? Beethoven was puzzled by this problem. In a letter to the Edinburgh publisher George Thomson, dated 19 February 1813, he asked:

Si à l'Avenir entre les airs que vous serez dans le cas de m'envoyer pour etre composés il y avait des Andantino, je vous prierais de me notifier si cet Andantino est entendu plus lent ou plus vite que l'Andante, puisque ce terme comme beaucoup d'autres dans la musique est d'une signification si incertaine que mainte fois Andantino s'approche du Allegro et mainte autre est joué presque comme Adagio.

(If in future among the airs which you will be sending me for setting there were some Andantinos, I would ask you to let me know if this *andantino* is to be understood as slower or quicker than *andante*, since this term, like many others in music, has such a vague meaning that often *andantino* comes near to *allegro*, while at other times it is played almost like *adagio*.)

Presto means literally nothing more than 'quick, prompt', but it came to be understood as faster than *allegro* (lively) and has generally been used to indicate a very fast speed. Sometimes composers do not seem to understand precisely what they want and may even appear to ask for the impossible. Schumann, who, like Wagner and many other German composers, tended to use his native language, marked the opening of the first movement of his G minor piano sonata: *So rasch wie möglich* (as rapid as possible); but on the last page of the movement the pianist is instructed to play *noch schneller* (faster still).

*   *   *

How much variety there can be in the interpretation of tempo can be observed by listening to different recordings of standard works. A typical example is the first movement of Mozart's G minor symphony, which has been made to sound elegant or fiery by the adoption of contrasting tempi and also by different ideas about the expressive content. The numerical time-signatures used by composers of the past can often be misleading. The sign ¢, for example, does not automatically mean two quick beats in the bar; it merely indicates that the basic rhythm is two rather than four. Mozart, for instance, uses ¢ for the whole of the overture to *Die Zauberflöte* (The Magic Flute), both for the introductory Adagio and for the Allegro that follows. The speed of the Allegro, therefore, is not determined by any arbitrary considerations but by the character of the music itself. Too slow a speed will kill the urgency and vitality of the music: too fast a speed will blur the semiquavers which occur in the opening theme and frequently throughout the piece. In particular an excessive speed will make it difficult for the timpanist to articulate his semiquavers clearly in the final bars. This is one of many cases where a study of the details of a piece will help to determine what its overall speed should be. The overture to Wagner's *Die Meistersinger* is an instructive example. It is marked at the beginning: *Sehr mässig bewegt* (at a very moderate speed). After some minor fluctuations of tempo we come to the lively woodwind passage (in E♭ major) which is associated with the apprentices and is, in fact, a diminution of the principal theme of the Mastersingers. This is marked: *Im mässigen Hauptzeitmass* (in the moderate principal tempo) – in other words, the speed is exactly the same as the opening but it will sound twice as fast because quavers are used instead of crotchets. This relationship between the two versions of the theme is often obscured in performance: the opening is taken at a brisk speed, which is slowed down when we come to the apprentices because it would then be too fast. This is clearly contrary to Wagner's intention, which was that the whole overture should be in the same basic tempo. Here again the details of the music can provide a clue to the interpretation of *sehr mässig bewegt*. When all three principal themes are heard together the Mastersingers' theme is played by bass instruments, including the tuba. Whatever speed is chosen makes no difference to the double basses; but it does make a difference to the tuba-player, who has to breathe. Since at one point his part is marked *sehr gebunden* (very smooth) and there are virtually no gaps for breathing, too fast a speed will mean that the ends of his phrases will be severely clipped and the whole dignity of the utterance will be lost.

As a warning against excessive speed we often find the indication: *Allegro ma non troppo* (fast but not too much). As a warning it is useful, but it is no more conclusive than the simple indication *allegro*. If we do not know precisely what is implied by 'fast' we are not likely to be made more certain by being told 'not too fast'. It seems likely that the interpretation of the Italian terms has not always been consistent, quite apart from modifications of their meaning. Bach, according to his son Carl Philipp Emanuel, liked to set a lively tempo when he was conducting, presumably in quick movements, and we are not likely to go wrong if we attempt to do the same when performing his works. There

is no evidence that eighteenth-century musicians liked their music to be staid. The guiding principle is clarity. If there are a great many short notes – semiquavers, for instance – which sound rushed in performance, then the tempo is too fast. Special caution is needed with the indication: *Andante allegro*, found in Handel, for instance in the chorus 'For unto us a child is born' in *Messiah*. At first sight this seems a contradiction in terms, if we think of *andante* as meaning 'moderately slow'. A glance at the music, however, makes the sense clear. The quavers move fast and the crotchets in consequence move steadily. The basic tempo is moderate, but the general effect will be lively. Handel's autograph makes it clear that he was anxious that this movement should not be taken too fast: he originally wrote simply *Allegro* and added *Andante* afterwards. 'Every valley', which is often performed at a speed at which the singer has little time to articulate his runs, is actually a parallel case, though here the marking is simply: *Andante*. Once again the basic tempo is moderate, but the quavers will appear to move fast, and this, coupled with the frequent semiquavers for the soloist, will create an overall impression of liveliness.

Decisions about tempo are not made easier by conventions of notation, current in the eighteenth century and not yet abandoned, by which a movement with two minims to the bar (¢ or $\frac{2}{2}$) may be fast while one with three quavers to the bar ($\frac{3}{8}$) may be slow. In such cases speed is determined, in the light of indications like *allegro* and *andante* (if they occur), by the character of the music, as suggested above, and by the internal division of the beats. If it is dangerous to go too fast in an Allegro, it can be equally dangerous to go too slowly in an Andante. A slow speed can easily degenerate into something that is flaccid and lifeless. On the other hand, there are cases where an extremely slow speed is obviously intended by the composer and where any attempt to increase the speed will damage the character of the music. The opening section of Sibelius's seventh symphony is marked: *Adagio* (♩) and the time-signature is $\frac{3}{2}$ – three minims to a bar. The crotchet in brackets, without any metronome mark, indicates that this is the unit of measurement. When in due course the music moves into a solemn procession of three minims in a bar the crotchet is still the unit, which means that the movement is exceptionally slow. Awareness of this slowness may easily lead to the feeling that the tempo needs in some way to be animated; but there is no indication that the composer intended this, and for want of any such indication the conductor is bound to hold back the music to the tempo at which he began the movement.

Transitions between one tempo and another, once indicated precisely by proportional signs, may be made clear by the provision of new metronome marks or by simple indications that the minim of one section is equal to the crotchet of the next, or whatever the exact relationship may be. Where no such indications exist there may be a real problem in deciding what the relationship is between an Andante and a succeeding Allegro, or *vice versa*. It may be that the change of tempo is meant to be abrupt, in which case there is no problem; but if there is a direct and close transition between one speed and the next it will be necessary to find a relationship which makes the transition seem logical, without any exaggeration of either the new or the old tempo. Slowing up the tempo (*ritardando*) or quickening it (*stringendo*) also require a very careful judgment. If the change is too abrupt in either case there will be a kind of bump which will upset the natural flow of the music. The tendency to slow down at the end of a movement, even where this is not marked, is a natural one; but it does not follow that this is always effective. In a quick movement it can cancel the impression of liveliness created by the movement as a whole: in a slow one it can exaggerate a speed which may already be as slow as is comfortable or tolerable. Once again judgment is called for, and an acute ear. An interpreter who does not listen critically to what he is doing ought to leave music alone.

Expression

No one is likely to question the view that expression is an indispensable part of musical interpretation. Stravinsky's celebrated observation that music is incapable of expressing anything at all did not mean that he considered music to be inexpressive. The markings in his scores and his own performances of his works should make this clear. The interpreter's task is to find out what the music is saying in purely musical terms, without regard for any non-musical associations. This is equally true of vocal music, where strictly speaking the composer has interpreted the text and it is left to the performer to interpret the music – which does not mean that the words do not matter. A great deal of music of the past has only the barest indications of expression, or none at all. This extends to such a simple matter as dynamics. Bach, for instance, will mark the accompanying strings in an aria *piano* when the voice comes in, in order to secure a proper balance; and from this it is reasonable to suppose that the orchestra is to begin its introduction reasonably loud. Indications like *piano, più piano, pianissimo* occur from time to time in early eighteenth-century music to indicate a gradual diminution of the sound, but they are relatively uncommon. Their use goes back to the seventeenth century. A particularly notable example in English music is the 'Curtain Tune' in Matthew Locke's music for *The Tempest* (1675). This begins 'soft' and at intervals becomes 'lowder by degrees', 'violent', 'soft', 'lowd' and 'soft and slow by degrees'. Though the indication of such nuances came to be more precise in the middle of the eighteenth century, with the regular use of the terms *crescendo* and *diminuendo*, they were clearly not a novelty then. The traditional view that early eighteenth-century music was either loud or soft, often expressed in a reference to 'terrace dynamics', cannot be sustained. These simple contrasts were inevitable on the harpsichord and the organ, which had no power of modifying the sound; but other instruments were not restricted to them. It would in any case be very difficult to play the violin for any length of time without altering the dynamics. As for singers, they had long been taught to practise the so-called *messa di voce*, which meant increasing and diminishing the sound on a single note.

We may guess from what Frescobaldi says about rhythm in madrigal singing that gradations of tone were also employed in addition to the simple alternation of *forte* and *piano* to represent an echo – long a favourite means of expression in both vocal and instrumental music. The part-books used by madrigal-singers do not, however, record these subtleties. It was the development of solo singing with continuo accompaniment

at the end of the sixteenth century that led to a formulation of the principles of expression that a singer should observe. *Example 26* is an extract from the preface to Giulio Caccini's *Nuove musiche* (1602), the title of which suggests not only a new form of music but a new approach to interpretation, though no doubt the author is merely summarizing and illustrating methods that had been practised for some years before his book was published. (a) is a reproduction of the original, (b) a transcription of part of it into modern notation.

The instructions printed above the music may be translated as follows:

(1) 'Without a regular beat, as though talking in music with the neglect (of regular rhythm) mentioned above' (referring to an earlier part of the preface);

Example 26 (a)

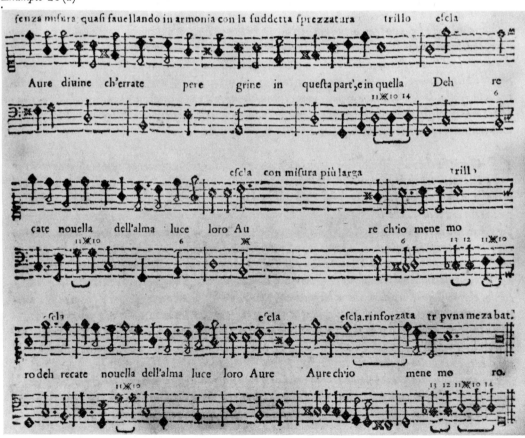

(2) 'Vibrato' (*cf. Example 14*);

(3) 'Exclamation', (i.e. a swelling or diminution of the tone, in this case a diminution followed by an increase in volume;)

(4) 'Exclamation in a broader rhythm';

(5) 'Vibrato';

(6) and (7) 'Exclamation';

(8) 'Reinforced exclamation';

(9) 'Vibrato';

(10) 'In a moderate [regular] tempo.'

Observance of these instructions does not exclude the introduction of ornamentation, as illustrated earlier in Caccini's preface.

Caccini intended his observations on interpretation to apply to the solo madrigals and airs printed in his volume. The detailed indications shown in *Example 26* hardly ever occur in these pieces, and this is quite natural, since a singer educated on Caccini's lines would be expected to know how to interpret them. It is noticeable that even when dynamics came to be marked with some regularity in instrumental music they were often omitted from a solo voice-part, presumably on the assumption that a singer should know instinctively how to interpret his part and that it would be unwise or unreasonable to tie him down too strictly. This was to some extent practical politics, since eighteenth-century singers, particularly in opera, tended to be a law unto themselves. This respect for, or subservience to, singers continued for a long time. Instrumental ensemble music was a different matter. From the middle of the eighteenth century onwards, with the growth of a more rigid orchestral discipline, dynamics began to multiply. Not only *crescendo* and *diminuendo*, but indications like *sforzando* (for a sudden accent) became common. Players were expected to do exactly what they were told and not to follow their instinct or tradition. But it was particularly in the nineteenth century that marks of expression proliferated, as composers became more and more conscious that their music was a form of subjective

(*b*) *Senza misura quasi favellando in armonia con la suddetta sprezzatura*

Au - re di - vi - ne ch'er - ra - te pe - re - gri - ne in que - sta part'e in quel - la, Deh re - ca - te no-vel - la dell' al - ma lu-ce lo - ro *etc.*

[6] [♯] [6] [♯] [6] 11 ♯10 14

6 11 ♯10 6 [♯]

*Possibly a misprint for

49

expression, in which every detail mattered. Their scores not only tell performers what to do but on occasion warn them what not to do. This is characteristic of Romantic music as a whole. Mahler, in particular, was fond of telling conductors not to hurry (*nicht eilen*) or not to drag (*nicht schleppen*). The traditional Italian terms, such as *maestoso* (majestic), *cantabile* (songful) and *con brio* (with energy) became augmented with scores of others in various languages. *Example 25*, from Elgar's *The Dream of Gerontius*, is a typical example of the care taken by a Romantic composer to ensure that every detail of his music is performed exactly as he imagined it. *Example 27* from Mahler's sixth symphony (1904) will illustrate how instructions of this kind can be applied to a whole orchestra.

The Italian terms used are traditional: *ritenuto* (held back); *morendo* (dying away, already used in the seventeenth century by Monteverdi); *espr.*, abbreviation of *espressivo* (expressive); *marcato* (accented); *arpeggiando* (spreading the chords); *sempre f* (still loud); *dim.*, abbreviation of *diminuendo* (getting softer); *sempre p* (still soft); *pizz.*, abbreviation of *pizzicato* (plucked [with the fingers]); *arco* ([with the] bow). The German terms, some of them equally traditional, extend the vocabulary: *Langsam* (slow); *schleppend* (dragging); *Viertel* ([with the] crotchet [as unit of the beat]); *wieder etwas fliessender* (again a little more flowing): *langsame Halbe* (slow minim, i.e. two slow beats in the bar); *Zeit lassen!* (leave time, i.e. do not hurry the piccolo, first oboe and the three clarinets); *Flag.*, abbreviation for *Flageolett* (harmonics, produced by lightly touching the string at the half-way point, producing a clear sound an octave higher); *Resonanz* (play near the soundboard); *mit Dämpfer* (with mutes). In addition there are combinations of German and Italian as warning indications: *mf aber marcato* (moderately loud but accented – unnecessary since there are accent signs over the notes); *nicht arpeggiando* (do not spread the chords). Very little is left to the conductor's initiative or to the instinct of his players, though the first horn may be presumed to have his own ideas about the

interpretation of *espressivo*. *Example 28*, on page 53, from Schönberg's *Kammersymphonie*, Op. 9 (1906), is a further illustration of detailed directions, though these are less fussy than Mahler's.

In addition to frequent indications of *crescendo* and *diminuendo*, represented by the signs ⟨ and ⟩ , the sign ♩ = ♩ is a reminder that the crotchet beat in the $\frac{6}{4}$ bar is the same as in the previous bar (not shown). The German terms are: *etwas bewegter* (*fliessender*) (rather faster, more flowing); *Bogen* ([with the] bow); *Dämpfer weg* (mutes off); *sehr weich* (very gentle); *ohne Dämpfer* (without mutes, unnecessary in view of the previous instruction); *am Frosch* (with the nut [end of the bow]). Note also the marking *sfp* (*sforzando piano*) – a sudden accent on the note, which immediately becomes soft.

The profusion of signs in late nineteenth- and twentieth-century music might be taken to suggest that the interpreter has very little to contribute. This is not so. It has been said that all one has to do with Elgar's music is to observe all the markings and the result will be what he intended; but in fact Elgar's own performances had an individual quality which has been captured only by conductors like Landon Ronald and Adrian Boult, who not only knew the composer well but had a sympathetic understanding of his music. A performance of one of Elgar's symphonies which merely follows the expression marks in the score can easily sound brash or vulgar. The soul of the music lies behind the external evidences of its existence. With older music the problems of expression are as acute as those of tempo and phrasing: indeed, all three are related. In many cases the interpreter has to start from the beginning and decide where the music should be loud and where it should be soft and where gradations are appropriate not only between these limits but above and below them. The legendary piano-teacher who said to her pupil: 'Don't put in the expression, dear, until I tell you' was sadly mistaken. Expression cannot be divorced from technique. To take a simple example, the fingering of a passage on the piano may depend on whether

Example 27

it is to be played soft or loud. Similarly, expression decides which string a violinist uses when there is a choice between two.

These principles are clear enough but they do not necessarily offer a solution to individual problems. In so far as there is a solution it will depend to a large extent on the period when the music was written and the composer who wrote it. To play Bach expressively it is necessary to know his music intimately and to study his own marks of expression where these occur. This study should not be confined to music written for a particular medium. An organist can learn a good deal about phrasing from string-players and singers. That extremes of dynamics are by no means out of place in earlier music is evident from Matthew Locke's use of the word 'violent' in his 'Curtain Tune'. It is true that this occurs in music for the stage, but throughout the seventeenth and eighteenth centuries there was a close link between the theatre and the concert room: there is, for example, an obvious interaction between Mozart's operas and his instrumental music. No one need be afraid of a dramatic interpretation of the symphonies of Haydn and Mozart, under the mistaken impression that Beethoven was the first to impart this quality to instrumental music. The very perfection of a good deal of instrumental music of the past may mislead the interpreter into thinking that its principal qualities are elegance and a kind of virginal purity. Finding the right expression means discovering the passion beneath the surface.

In music nearer our own time the details of expression are often set before us so clearly that all that is needed for their execution is judgment. One instance is the use of the sign < > to signify a *crescendo* followed by a *diminuendo*. A few exceptionally conscientious composers indicate the dynamic level at which the *crescendo* stops. Others leave this uncertain. If the music is marked *piano* before the *crescendo* begins, is the culminating point to be *mezzo forte* or *forte*, or possibly even no more than *mezzo piano*? The words

Au piano *Pierre-August Renoir, 1892*

poco or *molto*, which are sometimes inserted, will tell us whether the *crescendo* is to be little or much; but more often than not they are absent. We are left with a choice ranging from a gentle swelling to a passionate outburst. The decision depends on a variety of factors: on the length of the *crescendo* and *diminuendo*, on the speed of the movement, on the context and on the character of the music at that particular point. But there still may be uncertainty. In *Example 28*, from Schönberg's *Kammersymphonie*, the direction *sehr weich* in the string parts in the third bar may be assumed to imply a gentle *crescendo* and *diminuendo*: in any case there is hardly time for much more, seeing that the chords begin *pianissimo*. In bars 4–6 of the woodwind parts we have a passage which begins *piano* and in the flute and first clarinet presumably ends *pianissimo*, to judge from the *pianissimo* marked in the second clarinet and the bassoon. All the players concerned, however, make a *crescendo* from *piano* to *piano* – a

Example 28

favourite device of composers to produce a sudden drop in the volume. But how loud should they be playing when they reach the double bar; and how big is the *crescendo* to be in the third bar? There is nothing in the score to tell us: this is a matter that the interpreter has to decide for himself.

Performers

Of all interpreters the singer probably has the hardest task. For one thing, his instrument is part of his body and is subject to the imperfections and ailments that all human beings have to endure. For another, he is concerned not merely with the production of a sensitive and expressive vocal line but also with the enunciation of words. Singers who are supreme masters of the vocal line are not always equally successful with words, and *vice versa*. The two are actually inseparable, since correct enunciation of the words can colour the vocal line and the way in which the music is sung can give emphasis to the words. For physiological reasons, which we need not go into here, the deeper the voice the easier it is to make the words clear: sopranos find it more difficult than basses. It might be argued that in many operatic arias, particularly those of the eighteenth century, the intelligibility of the words is not of prime importance, since they are frequently repeated and being in Italian in any case are not likely to be understood by a non-Italian audience. Metastasio, the high priest of the Italian libretto in the eighteenth century, would hardly have agreed that his poetry did not matter. Even if we discount his opinion as irrelevant, it would seem that there is not much point in singing words if no one can understand them: the logical thing to do would be to utter some kind of mumbo-jumbo – a view which some contemporary composers appear to share. Given, however, that the words matter, there is still the question of what emphasis they should receive. Composers often have their own views of which words are the most

important and translate these views into their settings. A singer who concentrates on communicating the words at the expense of the music may run counter to the composer's intentions. The ideal interpretation is one in which music and words appear to be fused indissolubly into one. None the less there are in certain types of music conventions which have nothing to do with the words and virtually ignore them. This is particularly true of the culminating top note in many operatic arias. Nineteenth-century composers expected singers to dwell on a top note in this context, since brilliance of tone and the virtuosity displayed in sustaining the note would add considerably to the dramatic effect. It is not certain that they would have approved of the sustaining of any top note, irrespective of its context, as singers often do at the present day. Ernest Newman once suggested that a soprano who wished to demonstrate her capacity for sustaining a high note should come on to the platform, sing a top C, and then get on with the programme without the distraction of introducing such a display in places where it was not appropriate. This suggestion is not one that is likely to be generally adopted.

Like all interpreters, the singer needs a sense of style and period. It is a pity that singers, as a result of their teaching, so often rely on out-of-date editions of early music, believing that what they see in print must be right, and expect their accompanists to play every note of a defunct editor's interpretation of a figured bass. Unfortunately it is not only out-of-date editions that are misguided. There are at the present day editions of the vocal music of composers like Monteverdi and Purcell which indulge in such wanton elaboration that the accompanist seems almost more important than the singer, whose vocal line becomes a sort of Procrustean bed, with the measurements dictated by the accompaniment. A conscientious singer should not accept any edition of old music without taking advice from someone who knows the period, unless he is content to spend the rest of his career singing Mr. X's Monteverdi and Mr. Y's Purcell.

Seventeenth- and eighteenth-century composers would have expected singers to show initiative and to improvise their own ornaments and their own cadenzas. Ornaments have been discussed already. Cadenzas will be dealt with at a later stage.

* * *

Instrumentalists have their own problems, quite apart from the general ones which have been mentioned. Even if a violinist is not prepared to fit an eighteenth-century bridge to his instrument and play with a pre-Tourte bow, he should at least know something of violin-playing at this period and take the opportunity, when it occurs, of hearing what a reasonably authentic performance sounds like. Horn-players should accept the fact that their B♭ – F instruments can, by a simple manipulation of the valves, be turned into a tolerable counterfeit of a natural horn in A, G, E, E♭, D or C. Oboists should avoid playing Bach and Strauss in exactly the same way, though without committing the error of supposing that the former calls for an inexpressive style. Pianists need to know something of the difference between Beethoven's piano and their own and to be familiar with what is known of the style of playing favoured by composers as different as Mozart and Chopin. Organists cannot pretend to play Bach without understanding eighteenth-century conventions and registration: in particular they must know how to articulate and how to phrase.

* * *

The conductor has the responsibility for seeing that the forces which he directs produce a performance which corresponds to the pattern established in his own mind. Wagner said that the secret of conducting was to know where the melody lay; but as his own overture to *Die Meistersinger* has at one point three melodies heard simultaneously, it is difficult to accept his advice as comprehensive. There is in fact a great deal of music in which more than one melodic line is heard at the same time. It may be that one melody is more important than the others: Schönberg, followed by others, made this clear in his own music by labelling the principal part at any point *Hauptstimme* and any subordinate part *Nebenstimme*. There are also works where the relative importance of simultaneous melodic lines is indicated by contrasted dynamics. But there is a great mass of music where these distinctions are not made, and also works where a mere accompaniment is not marked as subordinate to the tune, though it obviously must be. Balance has to be one of the conductor's objectives, and in achieving the right balance he will achieve clarity. Precision of attack and exact chording may be taken as essential in any choral or orchestral performance, though they are not always secured, even in performances under conductors of repute. Those who can remember the performances of Mozart's operas which Fritz Busch conducted at Glyndebourne before the last war will recall the astonishment at hearing the two concluding chords of an orchestral recitative played exactly together.

Balance is not merely a matter of ensuring that the dynamics of each part of an orchestra are properly related to each other. It is also concerned, in older music, with the size of the forces engaged. It is not axiomatic that all eighteenth-century music was performed with relatively small forces. There are records of performances of Handel's oratorios in his lifetime with quite a considerable number of performers. Though most of the European courts had, from economic necessity, quite small orchestras, the opera at Milan had one which was quite substantial even by modern standards, and Mozart reports that he heard one of his symphonies performed by a very large orchestra in Vienna and thought it was magnificent – a fact ignored by people who speak of a 'Mozartian' orchestra when they mean a small one. At the same time it is true that most of Handel's oratorios and all Bach's church cantatas were performed by groups which would be considered very modest at the present day. One may assume in this case that the music was written with these forces in mind, and that is the strongest argument for using similar forces at the present day. The argument would be weakened if it could be shown that performances with a larger group would be equally, or more, effective. This depends on what is considered to be 'effective'. There may well be people at the present day who look back nostalgically to the monster performances of Handel's oratorios which were given in earlier years at the Crystal Palace in South London. The supreme moments in the more vigorous choruses were certainly exciting to listen to, but the loss of clarity was disastrous. We have precise statistics of the numbers of singers and players engaged in performances of Handel's *Messiah* in his lifetime. From these we know not only that the orchestra was of a modest size, but also that it was larger than the chorus, which incidentally was professional. A performance with forces balanced like this enables one to hear orchestral detail even in the most vigorous choruses – which is certainly not possible in the performances given by large choral societies. Until it is generally recognized that the orchestra in *Messiah* is just as important as the singers, audiences up and down the country will continue to revel in large masses of choral sound without realizing that this is not what Handel wrote. This evil tradition began with the Handel Festival in Westminster Abbey in 1784. It encouraged conductors to use editions in which substantial additions were made to Handel's orchestration in order to balance a large chorus and also to fill up his figured basses in the solos without being obliged to use a keyboard continuo.

Additions were at one time made to the orchestration of Bach's choral works, but these have long since been abandoned, either because they were found to be ineffective or because for some reason Bach's text was supposed to be more sacred than Handel's. Bach's works, however, have suffered from large choruses just as much as Handel's, though fortunately not from monster performances. The excuse sometimes put forward is that choral societies enjoy singing works like the *Mass in B minor* and the *St.*

Matthew Passion. But the enjoyment of performers can hardly be accepted as an æsthetic criterion. As with Handel, the clarity of Bach's part-writing is obscured if there is not a proper balance between choir and orchestra. Even with relatively small forces it is often difficult to ensure that the details of the orchestration are heard, particularly if comparatively gentle instruments like recorders have significant melodic lines. Bach had a long experience of orchestral conducting (he directed the *collegium musicum*, a mainly amateur body, at Leipzig for several years), and one would hardly be justified in accusing him of ignoring problems of balance. Such problems do, none the less, exist – for instance in the second Brandenburg concerto, where a recorder is matched against a trumpet, an oboe and a violin. In all music cases arise where it is necessary to subdue part of the orchestra in order to enable essential details to be heard. In the opera house it may often be necessary to subdue the whole orchestra, since composers tend to get excited at climaxes and forget that there are limits to the power of a single singer to dominate a *fortissimo* from trumpets and trombones. Paradoxically enough a chamber orchestra can do more to obscure a singer than a large ensemble. A single violin is more incisive than a group, and a smart rap on the side-drum can easily obliterate not only a soloist's words but the notes he is singing.

To the average member of an audience a conductor is a magician who by some unexplained power manages to persuade a large body of performers not only to produce an artistic result but to create a sense of excitement. The conductor's main work, however, is done behind the scenes. A perfect balance achieved in the concert room is the result not of frenzied gestures on the platform but of concentrated work at rehearsal. Many conductors – Wood and Beecham were among them – spend a great deal of time marking orchestral parts with dynamics which have been omitted by the composer or with nuances which are likely to give more definite effect to his intentions. Others, on the other hand, prefer to rely on detailed

Berlioz conducting

instructions in the rehearsal room. Toscanini is said to have accepted any set of orchestral parts that happened to be available. The character of his performances was the result of his ability to impress his personality on the players at a working session. Preparation of this kind is, needless to say, not the whole story. A concert creates conditions where a higher degree of excitement can be achieved by a conductor with the capacity for reminding the players at every point of what has been studied at rehearsal.

A concert should be an emotional experience for an audience, and in a sense it is also for the performers, whether they are soloists, conductors or members of an ensemble. But interpretation should never be subject to emotion: it must be controlled by the mind. The pre-requisites for a good performance are a warm heart and an ice-cold head. An actor on the stage cannot give a good performance if he himself is torn by grief or elated by joy. He has to analyse these emotions in relation to the character which he is portraying and then convey them to the audience: he must all the time know what he is doing and why he is doing it. In the same way a musician has to discover the emotional content of the music which he is performing and convey this to the audience by technical means. Beethoven wrote above the Kyrie of his *Missa solemnis*: '*Von Herzen – möge es zu Herzen gehen*' (From the heart – may it touch the heart). In the fulfilment of this wish the performer is, in the literal sense of *interpres*, the go-between, the means of transmission.

In the interpretation of choral music the conductor is dealing with a corporate body, where any expression of individuality from the members will adversely affect the total impression. His task is to unite a number of different individuals into a single entity. This is true to some extent of orchestral music: an orchestra must play as one. But it also includes a number of players, particularly wind-players, who have an individual role to play. These people are soloists in their own right within the corporate body. Though a conductor has to ensure that the performance as a whole reflects his ideas of what the interpretation should be, he has also to remember that the individual members of the orchestra are sensitive musicians who will respond to suggestion but may find it difficult to give the fullest artistic expression to a conception which is foreign to their own ideas. The wise conductor will be prepared to make concessions; and on a purely technical level he will realize that there are places where a finer interpretation will be secured by allowing some freedom to the individual. A horn-player, for example, may be able to bring a more complete artistry to the opening of Brahms's second piano concerto if he is allowed to start on his own when he is ready,

Strauss conducting   *Alois Kolb, 1924*

instead of waiting in a state of suspense until the conductor's stick falls. Similarly, at the beginning of Strauss's *Till Eulenspiegel*, where the horn has to negotiate a tricky passage and get faster at the same time, there will be a greater sense of ease if the conductor allows the player to make his own *accelerando*, provided that the final tempo has been satisfactorily established at rehearsal.

Concertos and vocal solos accompanied by the orchestra are a special case. It can happen that the soloist and the conductor have diametrically opposed views, in which case a consistent interpretation is impossible. One sometimes hears performances of a concerto where the soloist, on his entry, adopts a tempo markedly different from the one established by the conductor at the beginning of the movement. The only possible solution of this problem is compromise – or else the abandonment of any idea of collaboration.

Members of a chamber-music ensemble have to work in this way. Though the four string-players in a quartet may have worked together for several years, so that they instinctively know each other's reaction and tend to think alike, there is no guarantee that their opinions will always coincide. The conflict of views, if there is one, has to be thrashed out at rehearsal – temperately if possible, violently if necessary. The result of this process should be a performance in which all four players seem to be in entire agreement; in fact, they must actually be in entire agreement, however long and painful may have been the steps towards it. There are two principles involved here. One is the equivalent of saying that one does not wash dirty linen in public; the other is that the music always matters more than the performers.

Authenticity

Every honest performer believes that he is doing what the composer intended. Concert promoters sometimes go so far as to advertise 'authentic' performances, as though other people's were bogus. Authenticity is an agreeable ideal, but it is questionable how far it is practicable. In its extreme form belief in authenticity means that every work should be performed as nearly as possible as it was when it was first written. Against this belief is the contention that the prime purpose of performance is to give pleasure to a living audience. There are arguments against both these views. Those against authenticity derive from the fact that there is a great deal

Bohemian string quartet

Hugo Böttinger, 1929

that we do not know about methods of performance in the past, that not all the resources that were once used are available today, and that composers were not always particular about the resources to be used and frequently changed their minds when a work was revived. To take first our ignorance of the past, we have no means of knowing what kind of tone was used by singers at any period or what kind of tone was admired. When Chaucer writes that the Prioress 'entuned in hir nose ful semely' is he making fun of her or does he imply that a nasal tone was generally approved in fourteenth-century England? If we accept the latter do we extend it to cover all European countries and the thirteenth century as well as the fourteenth? The so-called 'Notre Dame' *organa*, of which a brief excerpt was given in *Example 1*, strike some people today as having an Oriental flavour. We know how Oriental singers sing at the present time. Assuming that they sang like this in the thirteenth century, did the chanters of Notre Dame in Paris copy them? The impossibility of answering these questions illustrates how the pursuit of authenticity can be frustrated at its very roots. As we have seen, we have some idea of the kind of ornaments that eighteenth-century singers improvised in opera and oratorio, and it is obviously admirable to make an attempt at reproducing them in a modern performance in order, at least, to recreate some of the brilliance and excitement that an eighteenth-century audience enjoyed. But what are ornaments without the tone that produced them? We have not even got the singers. In the seventeenth and eighteenth century *castrati* were among the most admired performers. We do not know what they sounded like, and for obvious reasons cannot experiment to find out. What is a present-day conductor to do when Handel and other opera-composers of the period call for a ringing, heroic, male soprano? A solution adopted in many modern revivals is to transfer the part to a tenor or, if the *castrato* was a contralto, to a bass. Unfortunately this effectively alters the whole character of the part, and it has deadly results when in the

original a soprano hero and a soprano heroine combine in a duet. In the final duet for Poppaea and Nero in Monteverdi's *L'incoronazione di Poppea* the two voices intertwine in a kind of voluptuous ecstasy which cannot be achieved by a soprano and a tenor (or baritone). Another example among many is the equally luxuriant duet *Per le porte del tormento* from Handel's *Sosarme*, sung by Elmira (female) and Sosarme (male).

When Handel could not find a satisfactory *castrato* he had no hesitation in giving male soprano roles to women. Though this was not a universal practice, it is probably the best solution at the present day, though something is inevitably lost in the adaptation. Another solution which has sometimes been adopted is to assign *castrato* parts to male altos (popularly known as countertenors, though the two voices are not identical). The objections to this are first the practical one that only a handful of male altos exist with the capacity to undertake these roles, and secondly that it is very improbable that the tone they produce is anything like the sound of a *castrato*. The problem of *castrato* parts arises in an acute form with Gluck's *Orfeo*. In Gluck's original Italian version Orpheus was sung by a *castrato*; today it has become almost a matter of tradition that it should be sung by a female contralto. To make matters more complicated Gluck rewrote the part for a tenor when a revised version in French was produced in Paris. The change of voice was not conspicuously successful, and attempts in later years to combine the two versions while retaining Orpheus's original part have been even less successful. An 'authentic' performance of the French version is, in a sense, possible; but it is not the best tribute to Gluck's genius. So far as voices are concerned the nearest approach to an 'authentic' performance of Bach's church cantatas is offered by the choir of St. Thomas's, Leipzig, which as in Bach's day is drawn entirely (trebles, altos, tenors and basses) from those *in statu pupillari* in the school. These conditions do not normally exist in England, so that even those who claim to give 'authentic' performances of the cantatas and the Passions have to compromise by employing a choir of adult men and women.

Instruments seem at first sight less problematical than singers. An enormous number of instruments have survived, either in perfect condition or capable of skilled restoration, from past centuries. Their sound can be discovered by experiment, instruction books exist to show how they were played, and craftsmen of the present day can make exact copies. The difficulty here is that exact copies are not always available, and even if they are, performers often avoid using them, either for economic reasons or on grounds of personal preference. Using a harpsichord to play the continuo does not automatically make a performance authentic, since if it is a modern instrument it will not produce the sounds to which eighteenth-century ears were accustomed. Even less authentic is the practice of using a harpsichord where it is the wrong instrument. It is still by no means uncommon to hear performances of Bach's *St. Matthew Passion* in which the Evangelist's recitative is accompanied by the harpsichord, under the false, though no doubt virtuous, assumption that this was the instrument that Bach intended. In fact there is no evidence that he used any other keyboard instrument than the organ in his church music. If we want authenticity in piano music we should use the instruments to which Mozart, Beethoven and Chopin were accustomed. If we want seventeenth- and eighteenth-century string music to have the ring of truth we need to worry less about instruments of the period, since many of these are available and highly prized; but as pointed out above we shall need to see that they have the right bridges and the right strings, and that the players use the right bows. Natural horns and natural trumpets (i.e. without valves) are also available, but only in relatively small numbers, and these are too often locked up in museums on the ground, which is indisputable, that they are beautiful to look at; and only a few players have developed a technique which enables performance on them

to be accepted without apology. Recorders are plentiful and should obviously be used where they are prescribed, with the proviso again that modern ones do not necessarily sound the same as old ones. Eighteenth-century woodwind instruments can be mastered with sufficient care, but it is worth recalling that they were not always completely mastered at the time. Charles Burney, visiting Mannheim, where the orchestra had a European reputation, wrote in 1773:

I found . . . an imperfection in this band, common to all others, that I have ever yet heard, but which I was in hopes would be removed by men so attentive and so able; the defect, I mean, is the want of truth in the wind instruments. I know it is natural to those instruments to be out of tune, but some of that art and diligence which these great performers have manifested in vanquishing difficulties of other kinds, would surely be well employed in correcting this leaven, which so much sours and corrupts all harmony. This was too plainly the case to-night, with the bassoons and hautbois [oboes], which were rather too sharp, at the beginning, and continued growing sharper to the end of the opera.

This is one of the cases where rigorous authenticity would defeat its own object. It would be a *reductio ad absurdum* to insist on out-of-tune playing in a modern performance.

Though there are many ways in which one can approach an authentic performance it would be a mistake to be too rigid about details. It is not axiomatic that recorder parts should never be played on flutes. Monteverdi has a piece in his seventh book of madrigals where recorders and flutes are offered as alternatives, and there is plenty of music of the past where similar alternatives are provided by the composer – violins instead of viols, for instance, or viols instead of trombones. Permissiveness was one of the characteristics of sixteenth- and seventeenth-century music, and some of it survived into the eighteenth century. Bach's keyboard music, other than that for the organ, is not specifically designed for any particular instrument, though some of it is clearly more suitable for the harpsichord than the clavichord. There cannot be any serious objection to playing *Das wohltemperirte Clavier* on the piano, provided that clarity is maintained. It is true that Bach did not like the pianos that he came across, but he did improvise a *ricercar* on one at Potsdam and took the trouble to write down his recollection of it afterwards. One should distinguish between what is permissive and what cannot under any circumstances be permitted. Re-scoring the music of Bach and Handel brings no positive advantage and does harm to the music. To say that either of them would have revelled in present-day resources is not merely to beg the question: it is a manifest absurdity.

In much of Handel's music there is considerable room for latitude in that he frequently made changes in his works when they were revived – not merely transferring a solo from bass to soprano, and so on, but also making cuts and adding new material, or else transferring music from one work to another. There is no such thing as an 'authentic' text of *Messiah*, since Handel made changes in it more than once. This has happened in later music too. Mahler was always. tinkering with his symphonies: to accept the latest version as the 'authentic' one leaves open the question whether he would have tinkered still more if he had lived longer. In Bruckner's case it was others who did the tinkering. Since this was apparently done with the composer's approval, it leaves open the question whether we are representing his ideas better by playing what he originally wrote or adopting the well-meaning suggestions of others. In our own time Stravinsky has produced new versions of some of his works in which the changes often go a good deal beyond modifying the instrumentation and changing the dynamics. We are not concerned here with the motive for these changes, only with the problem of deciding which of the two versions deserves to be regarded as 'authentic'. *Example 29* shows a single page of two versions of *Petrushka*: (*a*) was published in 1911, (*b*) in 1947. The changes here – in tempo, in

dynamics, in instrumentation, in the actual notes – can hardly be described as minimal.

No one will dispute that a performance which honestly tries to recreate as accurately as possible what is known about performances in the past is on the right lines. But nothing can alter the fact that the conditions of a modern performance are different. Both the performers and the audience live in a world with different associations; and however strong the passion for authenticity nothing can change twentieth-century human beings into the likeness of their predecessors. What is necessary in all music is to bring into focus what lies behind the notes. Beecham's performances of Delius's music were superior to the plodding and conscientious interpretations of some other conductors, because he took the notes at something more than their face value. Many of his interpretations of the music of other composers showed the same insight. After a performance of Vaughan Williams' opera *Hugh the Drover* which Beecham conducted the composer made a short speech in which he said: 'Sir Thomas assures me that he has not rescored the work, but it sounds as if he had'. This sense of 'newness' cannot be achieved by mere authenticity: it can come only from the exercise of creative imagination.

There is a good deal to be said for the view that one at least of the purposes of a performance should be to give pleasure to the audience – and not merely pleasure. After the first performance of *Messiah* Handel is said to have been complimented by Lord Kinnoul on the 'noble entertainment'. He replied: 'My Lord, I should be sorry if I only entertained them, I wish to make them better'. But whether an audience feels better after a performance or merely enjoys it is strictly speaking incidental. Since the interpreter's first duty is to the music, he may very well give a performance which will conflict with traditional views of what the music should be like. An audience which has been brought up on performances of *Messiah* with a large chorus and additional orchestration may be disconcerted when it hears one which adheres as closely as possible to what

Weber conducting at Covent Garden

Handel had in mind. Conversely a performance which gives immense pleasure to a large number of people may be not only historically but æsthetically wrong. The argument for a 'historically correct' performance is not that it is correct but that the music sounds better, provided the performers bring to it as much fervour and imagination as they would to music of a more recent date.

Improvisation

Two points related to interpretation remain to be considered: one is improvisation, the other is deportment. The improvisation of ornaments has already been discussed: in this case the interpreter is not adding anything new but merely amplifying what is implied in the music. But there is also a long-standing tradition of improvising at a final cadence material which, whether it is related to what has gone before or not, is new in the sense that it was not written down by the composer. The Italian word for cadence is *cadenza*, which came to be accepted in all countries as the technical term for this kind of improvisation. Since the *cadenza* is not merely an opportunity for a soloist to show virtuosity but is also the crown of the movement, the normal place for it in the *da capo* aria of the early eighteenth century was at the end of the repetition of the first section after a contrasted middle section. To have introduced it earlier would have been inartistic and would have weakened the sense of triumph with which the singer

Example 29

finished the aria and then, in opera, left the stage. The nature of the *cadenza* would depend a great deal on the type of aria to which it was added. A brilliant exhibition of fireworks would hardly be appropriate in a piece of a pathetic or reflective type; but where the aria itself demanded considerable virtuosity, the *cadenza* was an opportunity for the singer to show that he had a capacity even beyond the demands made by the composer. It was natural that this type of improvisation should be extended to instrumental music, particularly as improvising in general, or on a ground bass, had long been a practice of instrumental players. The length of a *cadenza* should be governed by good taste and judgment. When the violinist Matthew Dubourg eventually reached the end of an exceptionally long *cadenza* Handel is said to have remarked: 'Welcome home, Mr Dubourg' – which suggests that he was not entirely pleased.

Keyboard players were accustomed to improvise alone for their own pleasure or the astonishment of an audience; but since the keyboard concerto was a novelty in the early eighteenth century, there was no established tradition of what a *cadenza* in such a work should be like. No doubt this was why Bach, in the first movement of the fifth Brandenburg concerto, wrote out in full what is, in fact, a *cadenza* for the harpsichord. Keyboard improvisation could also be interpolated in other places. In the orchestral introduction to Armida's aria *Vo' far guerra* in Handel's opera *Rinaldo* (1711), the first he wrote for London, the music stops short at the beginning of the fourth bar and the composer merely writes 'Cembalo', indicating that he would improvise on the harpsichord at this point. In the same year the London publishers Walsh & Hare issued a collection of arias from *Rinaldo*, in which 'Vo' far guerra' includes 'the Harpsicord Peice [*sic*] Perform'd by Mr Hendel'. How far this is an authentic reproduction of what Handel played is uncertain: the probability is that he played something different at each performance. But, at any rate, it gives some idea of the lines which he expected an improvisation

to follow. In his *Ode for St. Cecilia's Day* (1739) opportunities for organ improvisation are offered in three places in the soprano solo 'But oh! what art can teach,/What human voice can reach/The sacred Organ's praise?'. And in his setting of *L'Allegro, il Pensieroso, ed il Moderato* (1740), the words of which are partly by Milton and partly by Charles Jennens, there are empty bars in the chorus 'There let the pealing organ blow', marked simply 'Organo ad libitum'.

Mozart and Beethoven both accepted the tradition of the improvised cadenza – naturally enough, since both of them were adepts at the art. It is true that Mozart actually wrote cadenzas for several of his concertos, but these were intended as models for others, not for his own use. There is no obligation on anyone to play them at the present day; but if the alternative is to use the numerous attempts made by later musicians to fill the gap, it is preferable to go back to Mozart, unless the player has the gift of improvisation and can offer something acceptable out of his head on the spur of the moment. In the course of the nineteenth century the tendency was to avoid the risk of unsuitable cadenzas by providing something ready-made. Mendelssohn wrote his own *cadenza* for his violin concerto and Schumann did the same in his piano concerto. Brahms' violin concerto, with the traditional place left for an improvised *cadenza*, is a late survival of the old tradition. By writing their own cadenzas composers were able to integrate them more closely with the rest of the movement to which they were attached. In his violin concerto Mendelssohn placed the *cadenza* not at the end of the first movement but in the middle and made it lead into the recapitulation. Elgar, in his violin concerto (1910), reserved the *cadenza* for the last movement and used it as a medium for nostalgic reminiscences of previous material: he also added a delicate and original orchestral accompaniment, with the string-players thrumming their instruments like guitars.

In recent years improvisation has taken on a new lease of life with the composition of works which leave the performers free to invent, either wholly or in part, their own material. Some of this do-it-yourself music has been written specially for school-children, who are thus able to exercise their imagination and at the same time are relieved of the necessity of learning elementary matters like keeping time. The freedom allowed to performers is not infrequently hedged in with precise instructions as to where they are to sit and where, if necessary, they should change places. A score of this kind may contain only a minimal amount of actual music but at least a whole page of marching orders. *Examples 30* and *31*, on pages 69 and 70, are extracts from two recent works in which considerable freedom is allowed to the performers.

Example 30 is from 'Pentomino' for wind quintet by David Bedford. In the first line the oboe is given a series of notes to play and is instructed to play them *staccatissimo* and as fast as possible, but the rhythmical organization of the notes is left entirely to the player. The second and third lines offer similar liberties, but with the precise duration of time indicated in seconds. After that the conductor beats time and the five instruments fit in the patterns assigned to them at the appropriate moments. They are then told to sit down. *Example 31* is the opening of a piece for a variety of instruments called *Module 1* by Earle Brown. Here only the raw material is presented. Module 1 runs to four pages, of which this is the first. There is also a second Module of the same length. The two Modules can be played separately or together. If they are played together, two conductors are needed. The directions include the following:

Each conductor of each Module must have an indicator with a moveable arrow which will inform the musicians of the *page* (1, 2, 3, 4) from which he will choose chords. . . . From any of the pages, the precise *chord* which the conductor has chosen is indicated to the musicians by the fingers of his *left* hand. . . . *All* chords are 'fermata' (⌢) : to be held by the musicians until specifically cut off by the conductor. . . . *Do not* physically separate the two groups : seat the musicians normally but distribute the parts so that alternate chairs have materials for alternate conductors.

There are also works published which have no music type at all: the players are expected to improvise from poems or diagrams of various kinds. A respected teacher of long experience and far from reactionary views recently asked a student who had written a work of this kind: 'Do you like other people to write your music for you?' It was a pertinent question. It is possible that the answer was 'yes'. If this were the general view we should inevitably be entering a stage where the art of creation depended entirely on the interpreter and the composer ceased to have any other function than that of dropping hints. In the hands of an inspired player interpretation of this kind can be stimulating; but experience has shown that if the improvisation requires a number of players it needs rehearsal – in which case it is not a true improvisation and has, in fact, virtually been composed by the conductor or the players who form the ensemble. The solemnity with which activities of this kind are conducted in public is not always in proportion to the result obtained.

Deportment

Deportment on the platform might be thought to have nothing to do with interpretation. It can, however, have an adverse effect. Pianists have been known to grunt, conductors to sing. Violinists and singers are both liable to suffer from facial contortions. Couperin, in his *L'Art de toucher le clavecin*, gave some sensible advice on this subject:

A l'égard des grimaces du visage on peut s'en corriger soy-même en mettant un miroir sur le pupitre de l'épinette, ou du clavecin.

(With regard to making faces, you can correct this yourself by putting a mirror on the desk of the spinet or harpsichord).

Three young musicians

Jan Miense Molenaer, 1629

He would have approved of a seventeenth-century amateur, Susanna Perwich, of whom her biographer wrote in a memorial volume:

> No *Antick* gestures, or bold face,
> No *wrigling* motions her disgrace . . .
> With body she ne're sat *ascue*
> Or mouth *awry*, as others do.

A different picture is presented by Burney's account of his visit to C. P. E. Bach:

After dinner, which was elegantly served, and chearfully eaten, I prevailed upon him to sit down again to a clavichord, and he played, with little intermission, till near eleven o'clock at night. During this time, he

grew so animated and *possessed*, that he not only played, but looked like one inspired. His eyes were fixed, his under lip fell, and drops of effervescence distilled from his countenance.

It is only fair to point out that this was a private occasion; but one cannot help wondering if Bach also behaved like this when giving a public performance. Beethoven's manner at the keyboard was very different, according to Czerny, who was his pupil:

His bearing while playing was masterfully quiet, noble and beautiful, without the slightest grimace.

Example 30

Flt, Clt, Hrn, Bsn tacent. Conductor tacet, the timing is up to the soloist

✳ in this passage (and in similar passages for the other instruments) the player should attempt to give the impression that the high note doesn't stop while the lower ff notes are played

Example 31

MODULE I

EARLE BROWN

This is a model that many performers might copy. Unfortunately there are members of the public who believe that a performance cannot be significant unless there is a physical display of involvement: the conductor's arms must fly here and there in wild gestures, the pianist must shake his head from side to side like a dog worrying a bone, ferocity, tenderness and pain must chase each other across a singer's face. There is, of course, a distinction here. A singer, even when not on the stage, is an actor, and for him to give no sign that he understands and appreciates what he is singing would, in a public performance, be disconcerting. At the same time, it is undeniable that one can derive immense pleasure from listening to a singer on a record or on radio, where there is no physical contact. What is certain is that extravagant mannerisms from any performer are no aid to interpretation and may fight against it. Self-control on the platform is as necessary a part of a performer's education as learning the notes and understanding the style.

The mechanics of interpretation are complex and often frustrating: the result to be achieved is comparatively simple. One could imagine an ideal world in which there existed one, and one only, interpretation of every piece of music. It might be an ideal world but it would be a very boring one. Part of the fascination of listening to music is the realization that X's interpretation and Y's can be equally valid, provided they have both approached the music with the same honesty, the same care, the same humility and the same sincerity. Equally X may give interpretations which vary slightly from one occasion to another. It is the great, and possibly the only, defect of the gramophone record that it makes permanent a particular performance, or a performance assembled from a variety of tapes. A performance should be a unique occasion. It is the interpreter's business to see that it is.

Book List

BOYDEN, David D., *The history of violin playing from its origins to 1761* Oxford University Press, 1965. £8.20.
An encyclopaedic work covering every aspect of its subject and throwing a good deal of light on interpretation in general.

DART, Thurston, *The interpretation of music* Hutchinson, 4th ed., 1967. £1.50; paperback 60p.
The best introduction for the general reader, comprehensive in scope and offering a great deal of detailed information in a relatively small space.

DONINGTON, Robert, *The interpretation of early music* Faber & Faber, 2nd ed, 1965. £6.50.
An essential work for everyone who wants to perform seventeenth- and eighteenth-century music. Too detailed for the general reader if read in bulk but a mine of information for anyone who is willing to dip into it with the aid of an excellent index.

HARDING, Rosamond E. M., *Origins of musical time and expression* Oxford University Press, 1938. o.p.
A series of essays describing how tempo and expression marks came into general use and providing a history of the metronome and its predecessors.

STRUNK, Oliver ed, *Source readings in music history* Faber & Faber, 1952. £5.25.
An anthology of writings on music, translated into English. It includes composers' prefaces and supplies a fair number of texts from which conclusions about interpretation can be drawn.

N.B. The works by Quantz and C. P. E. Bach cited in this book are available in English translations.

Acknowledgment is due to the following for pre-mission to reproduce illustrations:

ARCHIV FÜR KUNST UND GESCHICHTE Liszt at the piano by Danhauser, page 43; BÄREN-REITER-VERLAG, KASSEL Musical example 10(*a*), page 19, 'Walther's *Lexicon*' page 21; BIBLIOTECA MEDICEO-LAURENZIANA (photo S.C.A.L.A.) Musical example 1(*a*), page 9; BIBLIOTHÈQUE NATIONALE, PARIS Marriage procession, (MS. fr. 12, 574, f. 113) – frontis-piece, Musical example 2(*a*), page 10, Psalmodia Christiana, page 31; BRITISH MUSEUM Musical example 14(*a*); CZECHOSLOVAK NEWS AGENCY Bohemian String Quartet, page 59; BREITKOPK UND HARTEL V.E.B, Toscanini by G. Tabet (from 'The History of Music in Pictures' by Georg Kinsky) – front cover; GERMANISCHES NATIONALMUSEUM, NÜRNBERG Musical Rehearsal, page 18; KUNSTSAMM-LUNGEN DER VESTE COBURG 'The Singing Master' by Richard Earlom, page 17; LIBRAIRIE HACHETTE Berlioz caricature, page 57; MANSELL COLLECTION The Violin Player by Dou, page 38, Au Piano by Renoir, page 52; NATIONAL GALLERY, LONDON The Concert by Lorenzo Costa, page 22, Two Boys and a Girl Making Music by Jan Molenaer, page 68; ÖSTERREICHISCHE NATIONALBIBLIOTHEK Richard Strauss, page 58; OXFORD UNIVERSITY PRESS Holding the Violin (both plates), page 40 (from 'A Treatise on the Fundamental Principles of Violin Playing' by Leopold Mozart, translated by E. Knocker); PENNSYL-VANIA STATE UNIVERSITY PRESS Cantors of the Volto Santo, page 8 (from 'Music and Art in Society' by François Lesure); RADIO TIMES HULTON PICTURE LIBRARY Weber conducting, page 63; UNIVERSITY OF GLASGOW Musical example 26(*a*), page 48; YALE UNIVERSITY MUSIC LIBRARY Musical example 16(*a*), page 30.

BOOSEY AND HAWKES MUSIC PUBLISHERS LTD for *Petrushka* (Stravinsky); NOVELLO AND CO LTD for *The Dream of Gerontius* (Elgar); UNIVERSAL EDITION (ALFRED A. KALMUS LTD) for *Chamber Symphony* (Schönberg); UNIVERSAL EDITION (LONDON LTD) for *Pentomino* (Bedford) and *Module 1* (Brown).

The cover illustration shows the conductor Toscanini, by G. Tabet.

© Jack Westrup 1971
First published 1971
Published by The British Broadcasting Corporation
35 Marylebone High Street WIM 4AA
Printed in Great Britain by
Lowe & Brydone (Printers) Ltd., London

SBN 563: 10352 3